THE MAGICAL WORLD OF TREES

They Love, Nurture and Communicate

DEBORAH CUNNINGHAM BURST

The Magical World of Trees
Copyright © 2017
All rights reserved

Printed in the United States of America
First Edition

Interior design by Deborah Burst
Cover design by Becky McGraw, Cover Me Photography and Design
Top cover photo by Christy Fitzmorris
Photos copyrighted by Deborah Burst unless noted

Published by Cloud Burst Publishing
www.deborahburst.com

No part of this book may be reproduced in any form or by any electronic or mechanical means, including information storage and retrieval systems, without written permission from the author, except for the use of brief quotations in a book review.

Please purchase only authorized electronic editions and do not participate in or encourage electronic piracy of copyrighted materials.

❀ Created with Vellum

To Greg Guirard, the Cajun Tree Whisper

To my mother, Helen Cunningham

To Kerry Burst, Pioneer of OIP Wooded Kingdom

Forever in My Heart
Rest In Peace

ALSO BY DEBORAH BURST

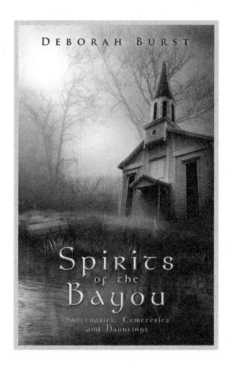

Hallowed Halls of Greater New Orleans

Louisiana's Sacred Places: Churches, Cemeteries and Voodoo

Southern Fried & Sanctified: Tales From The Back Deck

Spirits of the Bayou: Sanctuaries, Cemeteries and Hauntings

.

FOREWORD

My life has forever been changed in four delightful reads. The seed in writing this book began while listening to an NPR interview with Peter Wohlleben, German forester and author of the book *The Hidden Life of Trees*. If you love trees, you will love this book, highly recommended.

The second book, *The Nature Fix* written by Florence Williams, an award-winning author and journalist, touched me in many ways. With a relentless drive and passion, she traveled the world gaining evidence in the restorative benefits of nature. Her book not only proves her hypothesis but also confirms my own life-long belief that nature is the cure.

In doing research I returned to my lifelong mentors including the majestic Henry David Thoreau. It was then I discovered Richard Higgins' new book, *Thoreau and the Language of Trees*. A lauded writer, editor and journalist, Higgins transports the reader deep inside Thoreau's heart and soul.

Finally, the iconic Annie Dillard and her Pulitzer Prize-winning book, *Pilgrim At Tinker Creek*. Published in 1974, it is a book that stole my heart. She, like me, has a passion for writing literary nonfiction along with a deep love for forests and all the creatures that live there.

You can hear the child-like obsession, that gleeful spirit, but, like me, she doesn't hold back with a peppered honesty that refuses to bow down. I've read the book twice, and have begun my third read; it's that kind of book.

I gained much inspiration and guidance from my continued walks in the woods. Be it nature's calling or a mystical miracle; there also came a heightened awareness of conversations from loved ones who have passed. I've resurrected those lessons and pay tribute to their dedication in preserving our mighty forests.

Soon the environmental legends of John Muir and Ansel Adams found their way to the pages of the book, and I spent much time in reacquainting myself with their discoveries. They too deserve a prominent reference; their influence continues to be a driving force to protect our sacred lands.

INTRODUCTION

The rapturous beauty of trees consumes our everyday life, but how often do we truly study them? Most witness that obvious blur of green while driving the highway, but do you walk among them, run your hands across their bark? For some, a tree was that eternal playmate and the forests a magical land where dreams came true. But do they hear our words? Do they feel our arms around them? And do they have feelings?

This book delves deep to find the answers. Trees are the lifeline of humanity and home to untold numbers of wildlife. They are ancient gods deeply rooted in multiple religions. And they have a language all their own.

The book begins in sharing the anatomy of these wooded wonders, how they breathe, think and communicate. Masters of their realm, they send forth their fibrous roots in search of nutrients and share their bounty with young and old. From the gracious arms of an oak to the skyscraper pines that touch the heavens, they are what Henry David Thoreau described as "the preservation of the world."

This book is a bible to those who live among the trees. Together we will travel beneath the earth in search of life, brain activity among the roots. It is there we will discover our woodsy neighbors experience pain and have memories.

Some may believe outer space is the final frontier, but recent forestry research has unleashed some astonishing finds. The term family tree has taken on a whole new meaning, the trees themselves have family members and there is an intricate balance of life between man and tree. Forests mimic much what we desire, to live, propagate and provide for others.

The chapter, Seasonal Secrets, delves deep inside the forest's internal thermostat. During the winter, their leaves lay buried in the tree's womb nourished by the dark confines of hibernation. Come spring, a communal resurrection begins as each tree summons its winter's bounty of nutrition. It quickly flows from the roots through the tree's fibrous membranes, like blood flows through our veins. Tiny egg-like nodules sprout from the branches and soon leaves emerge like a budding butterfly from its tightly knit cocoon.

This is my religion, my cathedral, and my pulpit. The trees and forests are nature's divine providence. In the Fate of the Forest and the Climate Change chapters, we learn the effect of mass urbanization, the changing climate and how our forests are fighting back. They are immortal with untold secrets much like their creator, they own their own dimension of time, and although they know us for a mere blip on their radar, we must devote our lives to their protection.

Scientists and researchers from all over the world are bringing forth evidence in the symbiotic relationship between trees and humans. In the Nature's Cure chapter, you will discover the healing power of nature, proof in both science and personal anecdotes; just a walk through a park lowers stress and boosts the immune system.

A book on trees wouldn't be complete without words of wisdom from environmental legends of Henry David Thoreau, John Muir and Ansel Adams. Inspired by their work, the latter chapters include essays written from my early years as a photographer in discovering

Louisiana's bayous along with a local hero who dedicated his entire life in preserving the wooded wonders inside the Atchafalaya Basin.

There is a thin line between reality and fantasy as creatives share their own version of saving the forests. From blockbuster books to film and television adaptations, scenes of The Narnia Chronicles, Lord of the Rings and the Game of Thrones bring to life the mystical magic of trees. And to top things off, a fairy tale comes true with the discovery of a buried treasure, an ancient forest at the bottom of the Gulf of Mexico.

And what better way to close this magical journey than a chapter on the great forests of the world. From America's towering sequoia and redwood forests to the European rainforests filled with vast numbers of medicinal cures. There is so much to learn and this book is dedicated to those who seek answers, to the soldiers who fight to save nature's kingdom, and to you, the messenger who carries the soulful spirit that lives inside every tree.

New Orleans City Park Couturie Forest

WOODED WONDERS

Henry David Thoreau was so endeared with pine trees he proclaimed, "Like great harps on which the wind makes music. There is no finer tree." He further compared them to humans, "The trees indeed have hearts. The Pines impress me as human. Nothing stands up more free from blame in this world than a pine tree."

They are slender giants gracefully dancing at the whim of nature's mood. It is a tree that demands a different view, laying on a bed of grass and gazing above staring at its heavenly performance. That soulful sway in tune with its very own music as the wind slices through its nimble needles. What a wondrous creature, enamored by those who worship its beauty, and those who worship its lumber.

Tammany Trace Trail in Southeast Louisiana

As a fan of Thoreau and living more than thirty years on six acres of woods surrounded by another forty acres of forests, I share his affection for pine trees. Here in my home state of Louisiana, thirty-five miles across Lake Pontchartrain are the piney woods of what locals affectionately call the "Northshore." It is there the acidic soil feeds the ten-story-high pines.

A thick forest protects its core, but the lone pine is no match for tornadic winds that snap the wooded titans like toothpicks. Thoreau offered his own assessment, "The wind is making passes over them, magnetizing and electrifying them. As if in this windstorm, a certain electricity was passing from heaven to earth through the pines and calling them to life."

Fearful of their mighty weight, some homeowners elect to decimate these lovely creatures. And with no regard to the time of year, they cause even more harm.

Walking my wooded neighborhood, I pass a huge pile of freshly cut pine trees with long strands of sap dripping across their rings. Dozens of trees massacred during the height of spring, filled with bird nests and rising nutrients to the newly formed branches. Moving closer I could smell the fresh pine, like its last gasp for air; I sensed this was its final hour. And I cried, just as they were crying, these poor defenseless trees killed during their prime.

How ironic I should find a passage titled "Turpentine Tears" from Thoreau himself in a book written by Richard Higgins called, *Thoreau and the Language of Trees*. In a journal entry from March 1855, Thoreau witnessed a hillside of pines laid in waste noting what he called the crystal drops of turpentine dripping down the sawed ends of the tree trunk.

"...thickly as a shield, as if the dryads or pinewood nymphs had seasonable wept there at the fall of the tree. The perfect sincerity of these terebinthine drops, or drops of dew heaven-distilled and trembling to their fall, is incredible."

Another entry posted in December 1851, Thoreau saw two men cutting down one of the biggest pines near Walden Pond. He was infuriated, like beavers, he said, "...insects gnawing at the trunk of this noble tree." He watched as the lumberjacks inched their way, first with the saws, a time staking task gutting the thick wood, years and years of growth. Soon came the ax to open the sawed-crevice even more, and then the saw digging deeper into the flesh of the tree.

Stunned, Thoreau continued to watch, thinking with every move the tree would finally give up, surrender to this hideous chaos. But the tree fought hard, determined to win the battle. To stand tall, its branches grasping to feel that last final breeze, the warm sun glistening on its needles, and the baby squirrels hanging on for dear life.

Thoreau watched as the tree gasped its last breath, and penned this journal entry:

"How slowly and majestically it starts! As if it were only swayed by a summer breeze, and would return without a sigh to its location in the air. And it fans the hillside with its fall, and it lies down to its bed in the valley, from which it is never to rise, as softly as a feather, folding its green mantle about it like a warrior, as if, tired of standing it embraced the earth with silent joy, returning its elements to the dust again. There now comes up a deafening crash to these rocks, advertising that even trees do not die without a groan. It rushes to embrace the earth, and mingle its elements with the dust."

He continues his journal post in a state of mourning. Asking why the church bells are silent, why there is no procession of mourners for this mighty soul. Thoreau paid his respects by visiting the felled tree. A testament to its glory, he measured the girth. As he spread the ruler across the stump, tears of sap streamed across the wood. The remains of the mighty monarch measured four-feet in diameter and 105-feet long.

It was more than a tree; it was the lifeline of a mass community, a spiritual icon worshipped by its wooded neighbors. It was home to the hawk that perched on its branches to spy the fish in the stream below, and to the squirrels who felled its fertile cones to bring forth a new generation. It was a guardian for all that entered its empire and brought peace to the hearts of man.

COMMUNITY OF TREES

Imagine the stories this oak could tell, the 800-year old McDonough Oak in New Orleans City Park. I for one see a wise matriarch. Her gnarly roots like thick veins crawling across the leaf-littered floor. Its thick body and sprawling arms playfully twist and turn. I run my hands across her rough skin and compliment her long locks of curly moss hanging from the branches. Like humans, each tree is different and all are connected.

Trees move at a much slower pace, a different dimension of time compared to human years. Perhaps that is why they live so long, avoiding the hustle and bustle of life. And trees protect their colony, they release toxic chemicals to combat pests and send pheromones to predators so they may devour the rabid insects. But it takes a village of trees to survive, like a woodsy brotherhood they need each other to develop microclimates. Trees living inside thick forests live much longer than isolated trees.

Perhaps our desire to hug a tree is because it has characteristics similar to a human and animal. *The Hidden Life of Trees* by author and German forester, Peter Wohlleben notes that trees shed skin cells in growing their bark and a break in their bark is as uncomfortable as a tear in our skin. A more obvious find is how the bark wrinkles with age especially noted in a live oak.

Wohlleben has done much research on the subject and scientists believe trees have brain-like structures on the tips of the roots. The entire root system is thought to hold centuries of experience, knowledge passed on through generations of trees, thousands of years in some cases.

A type of reincarnation was found in stumps of a spruce tree in Sweden that revealed evidence of multiple trees all grown from the mother tree, a family of trees from a single root system. Carbon dating of the roots measured the tree to be 9,550 years old but yet the shoots from the single trunk base were much younger. So you have several generations of a tree created from a mother tree, just as a family examines its family tree.

The same is noted in the Redwood National Forest as their website shares the life of a redwood. Nicknamed cloud sweepers they rise above the mist reaching 300-feet into the air. These mighty titans reproduce from a root burl along the base of the tree, it remains dormant until the parent tree falls ill or injured, and then sends chemicals to grow new shoots. The park notes these are in fact clones of the tree that died which will carry the wisdom of the ancient tree.

LANGUAGE OF TREES

Trees have a finite language, and their root system is a vast network as each tree carries enzymes delivering messages from warnings of pests and disease to delivering much-needed nutrients to the younger trees. It begins with a mother tree, usually the biggest tree in the forest, and the forest is her domain, and she is their matriarch.

Although it appears this piece of science has been circulating for nearly two decades; a video by Dr. Suzanne Simard, a professor at the University of British Colombia Faculty of Forestry, has ignited a renewed interest. Published four years ago, social media has given it new life. She and her graduate students set out on a mission inside the Douglas-fir forests of British Columbia.

In the video Simard hikes through a vast umbrella of fir trees shuffling her feet across a thick bed of ferns. She stops and crouches close to the ground, and reaches into the dirt with her bare hands exposing the roots and fungi, what's called Mycorrhizal fungi. With the dirt sifting through her fingers, she explains the tree's roots supply the fungus with carbohydrate energy needed to survive. In turn, the root cells and the fungus cells intermingle moving carbon and nitrogen to plants and trees across acres of forests.

Simard hikes to higher ground and places her hand on a massive tree in what she estimates to be five hundred years old. She calls it a mother tree, a dominant tree in the forest, basically the nucleus of the network. Just as the earth's entire biosphere is all linked together, so are the pieces and parts of the forest.

Think in terms of a human body and the tree's ball of roots as the brain. Simard explains it is sending millions of messages to other trees, both physically and metaphysically. It brings a unified structure along with diversity and resilience to the forest. Which allows its ecosystem to battle fires, disease and storms more effectively. Much in what was witnessed after Hurricane Katrina.

It has been proven that trees boost their defense system when a pest is present, and send chemical warning signals through the fungal network to other trees so they too can boost their immune system.

The chemical can go out as quickly as six hours after the presence of a pest.

Simard closed her lesson suggesting that man disrupts the legacy of forests not only when they decimate trees for developments, but also when they immediately clear trees after a disaster. The dead trees are still busy transferring nutrients to their babies, tiny sprouts emerging from the forest floor. It is a beautiful ecosystem, where even death serves a purpose, a valuable lesson for mankind, one that is often ignored.

Couturie Forest in New Orleans City Park

The root system manages all the chemical activity, in charge of storing the water in the winter and in the spring sending the nutrients back up to the branches to create leaves. But brains also have electrical impulses, which have also been measured. Still, how can we measure intelligence?

In Wohlleben's research, the book shares how the tree's brains contain molecules similar to animals. For example, if the roots encounter an obstacle, be it a toxic substance or impenetrable rock, it analyzes the situation, transmits the adjustment to the root tip which then changes direction. But what hinders much of the research is the tree's slow ride down the track of life.

Moving away from the urban regions, deep inside the forests, one can actually detect trees communicating. Be it the feathery willow seeds riding the breezes, or fragrant blossoms releasing scents. Fruit trees, for example, use this method to attract bees to pollinate. Color is another tool, just as humans are drawn to photographs, insects and birds are drawn to a buffet of colorful blooms.

So that makes three different lines of communication, olfactory, visual and electrical from the roots. What about sound?

Swiss Scientists have recorded trees screaming when they are really thirsty. Of course we can't hear it because it's on an ultrasonic level. Their research found a crackling in the roots and when they played it in the laboratory, roots from seedlings not involved with the experiment took notice. They heard it and responded, just as humans use sound waves to communicate.

If you place a stethoscope against the bark of the tree just as the leaves begin to sprout, you can hear the gurgling water rising from the roots to the branches. The roots are busy delivering water and nutrition stored through the winter. Swede Scientists took it one step further monitoring the tree at different times of the day. They discovered a soft murmur at night, what they believe could be tiny bubbles of carbon dioxide in the tree's narrow water tubes. Wohlleben's book admits there's more research that needs to be done but they believe it may be caused by an abundance of fluid in the trunk while the crown takes a break from daytime photosynthesis.

TREES EXPERIENCE PAIN

Trees are a living entity and they constantly fight to stay alive. They also experience pain and stress similar to humans. Research has shown that they are especially vulnerable to pain in the winter when they're sleeping. And if the insects weren't enough, animals do their share of damage. Deer have a ferocious appetite and with increased urbanization, their grazing fields are shrinking so they turn to the forests. There they feed on tree bark.

Waiting until night for cover, they begin gnawing near the base of the tree and pull away large strips of bark. But during the winter it's not that easy. Since the nutrients reside in the roots during hibernation, it leaves the tree quite dry and so it's difficult for the deer to pull the bark from the tree. They are then forced to tear away chunks of the tree for food.

Imagine the pain of someone biting into your leg tearing away flesh, trees experience similar pain, and for some trees it can be fatal. Similar to an infection, the open wound is consumed by what the book, *The Hidden Life of Trees*, explains is a large-scale fungal invasion that breaks down the inner wood. The tree may survive depending on the size of the wound, the age of the tree, and the density of its woodsy neighbors. As a long time forester, Wohlleben has witnessed trees surviving even the deepest wound if they live in an undisturbed forest where their bark is tough and dense. It takes longer for younger trees, as much as ten years to close the wound, while Wohlleben added the commercial forests often see more casualties.

Larger trees offer a comfy refuge for woodpeckers. We admire the beautiful birds that are often quite large and easy to spot since they peck away at the bark instead of seeking refuge in the leafy branches. Besides chipping at the trees for insects, woodpeckers also build a nest inside the tree to raise their young.

Some go the easy route looking for dead trees still standing, while others look for mature hardy trees and hammer away making a small hole in the bark. It's amazing to learn some of the most unlikely relationships in nature. Wohlleben explains that it would be virtually impossible for the woodpecker to drill deep into a healthy tree and build a home. Instead, they wait for the fungus to enter that initial opening and begin breaking down the bark. It's a win-win for the bird and fungi, but not the tree. Once the bark is softened, the woodpecker returns to finish the job.

Other woodpeckers, as noted by Wohlleben, build multiple entryways to their newfound home. Like separate bedrooms or maybe a room with a view. The renovation is ongoing because the fungi continue to grow and softening the wood which creates a mushy home. Like an unwanted houseguest, the woodpecker pecks away at the fungi mush but it's a losing battle. Eventually, the woodpecker's fledglings take flight and move away leaving the soggy home.

So, is the tree doomed? Over the years different birds move into the tree opening, some more patient species like the owl will wait several years for the opening to get big enough to move into their new home. As the tree continues to rot, more birds will drill the rotting wood and build more homes. Meanwhile, wood ants and beetles will join the party eating the fungi mush and laying their larvae. In fact, the tree becomes somewhat of a science project in itself, a skyscraper home to bats and owls whose excrement feeds generations of multiple species of beetles. And the circle of life goes on and on.

Even though the tree has no defense for the interior damage, it can work hard in patching its external wound by growing more bark. Depending on the number of openings and health of the tree, some trees can survive for another hundred years. Proof again why it's crucial we should leave our sick and broken trees standing, they are home to a multitude of birds and insects. I personally witnessed this metamorphosis after Hurricane Katrina as many of my trees were injured and became home to many species of birds.

A fallen tree still thrives feeding multiple species and a home for small animals of the woods. Couturie Forest in New Orleans City Park

The same could be said for a dead tree trunk. Wohlleben believes a dead trunk is as much alive as a live tree and has nicknamed them the Mother Ships of Diversity. Similar to the fungi ridden tree invaded by the woodpecker, the trunk also becomes a buffet ready to serve thousands of species of fungi for beetles and firefly larvae. The book points out that one-fifth of all animals and plants equal six thousand species.

Property owners who insist on maintaining a pristine forest and removing falling trees are in fact removing vital nutrients. By giving pests a multitude of feeding sources, odds are they will leave the healthy trees alone. And the same rule applies to a downed tree, nick-named a nurse log; it becomes a nursery for young trees of the same species. Another reason why it is so important that we not be so tidy with our landscapes, reserve a healthy section of woods and leave them alone. Let them mingle, both living and dead, an army of decom-posers feeding the future.

MAJESTIC GIANTS

Annie Dillard, a lauded author, and Pulitzer Prize winner for nonfiction, shares the same sentiment in the endurance of trees, espe-cially older trees. In her book, *Pilgrim at Tinker Creek*, she astutely explains that trees do not accumulate life; instead they are a dead-wood that keeps wrapping itself with a new coat. And she, like me, believe them to be immortal, vulnerable she says only to another ice age. Well, that and the almighty bulldozer.

Trees become smarter as they age, they have memories and learn how to survive wicked weather based on life's experiences. Such is the case of the giant sequoia. Dillard shares an amazing story in how the tree can even survive a fire, their wood barely burns, nearly fireproof. When the top of a sequoia tree was struck by lightning during a summer thunderstorm, it smoldered without any damage, and finally the fire was put out by a snowstorm in October. Perhaps lessons in evolution as these enormous giants have learned how to toughen their hide knowing the cooling snow of winter will douse the flame.

Giant sequoia forests grow on the western slopes of the Sierra Nevada in California. There are forty different groves throughout the Sequoia National Forest and each tree is a striking landmark rising 4,000 to 8,000 feet in elevation.

No matter the season, the sequoias never disappoint, many groves can be reached by road while others may require a more arduous hike. Boardwalks are located throughout the park, a sight that defies description, as if these creatures are from another world, another dimension of time.

The photo above taken by Jim Bahn, courtesy of Wikimedia Commons, shares what is said to be the largest tree in the world. Its name is General Sherman, a giant sequoia tree in the Giant Forest of the Sequoia & Kings Canyon National Park in California. The tree is estimated to be 2,000 years old according to a test conducted in 2012. It stands 274.9 feet high but is not the tallest tree; that title goes to the Hyperion, a 379.7-foot-tall redwood in California. The sequoia measures 52,500 cubic feet in volume, more than half the volume of an Olympic-size swimming pool.

Although it is the largest tree, it does not hold the record for the oldest tree. It's a middle-age sequoia compared to some that are 3,220 years old. According to the LiveScience website, the brittle texture of the wood is not a valuable lumber, but the trees were still logged extensively at the turn of the twentieth century. They once thrived across the northern hemisphere and now preserved in Sequoia National Forest and the Sequoia National Park.

The champion of these mighty warriors, John Muir dedicated his life in preserving these forests. He studied their history and questioned their shrinking forests, restricted to what he noted was narrow belts along the California mountain ranges. What he believed were remnants of the tree's grand ancestors and possibly on the verge of extinction.

Muir explained the genus was once common, flourishing throughout Arctic regions along with the interior of North America and Europe, but only two species survived the hardships of time, the sequoia on the western slopes of the Sierra, and the redwood along the coastal mountains of California with some groves extending into Oregon.

In chapter nine of his book, *The Sequoia and General Grant National Parks* Muir proclaimed the sequoia to be "Nature's forest masterpiece," what he believed grew from the seeds of ancient stock, a keeper of the past. God-like structures that defy all others, the sequoia stands proud casting shadows on trees that appear infantile.

More than beauty, the forests are critical in transpiration, moving moisture from the mountain clouds to the plains. The sequoia is a tree of life forever feeding the lowlands, Muir explained, a "never-failing spring." Evidence they must be protected, their demise presents a chain reaction of death, steams dry up, farms left scorched and the air doused with pollutants.

The LiveScience website does an excellent job in describing each grove and hiking levels. They all share the passion John Muir championed in protecting these gentle giants. Muir Grove is an excellent place to find solitude as the two-mile hike is less visited and travels across a high-density grove of mature sequoias with views of a creek gorge.

A photographer's dream, the Redwood Mountain Grove is especially dramatic during the fall as rich gold light heats up the deep red of the dogwood shrubs. It's the largest grove in the park with substantial old-growth sequoias. Some trees show burn marks on the lower portions of the bark, evidence in the success of prescribed burning to reduce forest floor that can cause great harm to these earthly monarchs.

Redwood National Park in California, photo by Ramakrishna Gundra courtesy of Wikimedia Commons

❧ 2 ❧
SEASONAL SECRETS

Blue Ridge Parkway near Humpback Bridge

Perhaps there is nothing so commanding than the change of seasons, a communal resurrection, a renewal of love and a time to contemplate. A time when we are most connected to our natural confines, we long to be close to her and consumed by her beauty. We are in harmony with all creatures on earth; they too are experiencing the same in the cycles of life measured in the changing seasons.

I believe an artist sees the world in a different light, literally. Almost an addiction, some say an affliction, but around every turn or a long stretch of highway, creatives focus on every minute detail; the early sun peeking through the morning haze and the late afternoon glow when nature bids farewell to another day. Every cool snap whispers memories of autumn's painted landscapes, it's nature's grand finale, her siren song, that seductive allure before winter's somber hibernation.

In *The Hidden Life of Trees*, the Hibernation chapter reminds us that trees are a living entity and although we take this for granted, knowing the struggle trees bear to stay alive will give you pause. A renewed appreciation for our forests, every single tree, every minute change, be it the sun's reflection against the bright green leaves or the thunderstorm beating the ground below, we feel as one and can hear their whispers of woe and celebration.

Have you ever noticed how trees look weary as late summer arrives, perhaps tired of fueling themselves with energy from the sun? They turn the sun's rays into sugar and enzymes storing it under their skin, their bark, just like a bear would do when hibernating. Trees are careful in storing just enough to feed during the winter but not too much as the liquid can freeze causing major problems, even death.

As the waning days of summer come to a close the trees are busy breaking down the chlorophyll from the leaves pulling back the nutrients into the trunk, a reservoir ready to feed the budding nymphs when the next spring arrives. Slowly the pigment is drained and the leaves begin another metamorphosis, what many believe to be their last hurrah. But how many leaf-peepers who clamor to witness autumn's waves of blazing color realize these leaves are in fact warriors? Their flashy dressing wards off aphids looking for a winter home. The pesky insects know the colorful trees are healthy and full of toxins so they search for the weaker trees.

Of course conifers don't have time to bother with such nonsense like dropping leaves or changing color, instead their needles are more coarse and protected by a waxy substance along with a good chunk of antifreeze. Consider it nature's way of bringing diversity to the world; the evergreen's towering branches cast great depths of shadows across the land. A forbidding beauty, a shadowy blackness lurking inside the shade of hemlocks, fodder for tales of mysterious creatures roaming their dark abode.

Which begs the question, why do deciduous trees repeat this laborious task year after year?

It appears to be a product of evolution according to the book, *The Hidden Life of Trees*. A more modern invention in terms of nature's timeline coming in around 100 million years ago opposed to the conifers with a mature 170 million years. It's all about the winter winds that can be quite violent at times. The trees drop the excess weight of their leaves similar to a sailboat dropping their sails. Combined with the added autumn rains the soil can become quite spongy weakening the tree's footing.

New Orleans Brechtel Park

The book continues to explain how the winter winds can pummel a mature trunk with a force of 220 tons of weight. By losing their leaves, the trees are more aerodynamic. Since each tree is shaped differently, the wind is distributed more evenly, first the branches then narrowing the force down to the thicker trunk. In fact, it is that graceful dance swaying back and forth that helps sheer the wind of the entire forest, especially with nor'easter and severe storms.

Lessons learned from tragedies such as hurricanes and flooding can bring great strides in urban planning. In working for a regional newspaper just north of New Orleans, I had the privilege of interviewing Matt Monahan, a resident of Slidell and locally licensed arborist who shared his perspective in how trees can be a homeowner's friends.

Trees provide shade, reduce air pollution, slow surface water runoff and reduce soil erosion. In addition to the atheistic beauty, trees offer wildlife habitat and reduce noise pollution as well. Hurricanes Katrina and Isaac destroyed more than 30,000 trees in Slidell, a northern suburb of New Orleans, resulting in a sixty percent loss of green space. Katrina ripped apart massive cedars and water oaks, while the century-year-old live oaks survived.

As noted previously, trees work together to protect each other in deflecting the wind. For a short time during Hurricane Isaac, Monahan sat on his porch and literally watched coastal trees like the bald cypress and live oaks shed the wind.

"The tree would twist and move with the wind, maybe one branch would break, you could literally watch the wind shift," said Monahan. "Those trees were designed to shed the winds. Live oaks and magnolias are coastal adaptive trees. I've been educating people on this, and it was amazing to see it actually work."

He further explained, "Loblolly pines have been here for centuries and when they lose their branches, the wind flows through the tops. Slash pines are not native coastal trees and most came down with Katrina."

Monahan added much of what has been repeated here in this book, the interrelationship between the trees work together in both the wild and urban forests. He added often times people plant a tree truly for its appearance with no regard to whether it is native or non-native. No matter the species, planting one lonely tree will be short-lived. Monahan said it may last for a good twenty years, but will likely be lost with the first strong storm.

Wohlleben pointed out in his book that tornadoes are a different story as the tree crowns are heavy with leaves during the height of the tornado season in the spring and summer. And since tornadoes are so rare the trees have little experience to defend themselves against the mighty winds. Another force of nature that is equally damaging is severe thunderstorms. Those quick heavy rains dump a deluge of water on the leaves in a quick span of time. Unlike snow that falls through the limbs, the rain is torturous.

Hurricane Katrina tree damage from tornadic winds

Lightning is even worse, the tall trees, especially pines act like a natural lightning rod. One day the crown is a bright green and within a week the tree is dead. I've witnessed this on my property, one thunderstorm struck two of my pines and days later the needles were brown. However, the trees still stand offering homes and food for multiple birds and insects.

Wohlleben shared a story that not only lays claim to nature's fury but also how trees are interconnected. In a strand of Douglas firs in Central Europe, one tree was struck by two lightning strikes, but fifty trees died. Unfortunately, these trees were connected to the victim underground for some life-saving sugar but instead they received deadly bolts of electricity.

HERE COMES THE SUN

Imagine all the work from just one tree in the course of changing seasons. Even more amazing, except for spring and autumn, most of its work is invisible to humans. As Annie Dillard points out in her book, every year a tree replaces ninety-nine percent of its living parts. During the spring water climbs up the tree in a brisk pace of one hundred and fifty feet an hour, in the summer it easily moves a ton of water every day. All the while, the bark is twisting and turning, splitting and stretching, and spitting out new leaves, as many as six million leaves on one tree in what seems to be effortless.

They really don't ask for much, water and sun, and maybe a hug every now and then. And like everything in nature, it is the survival of the fittest.

Many of us are well aware of how important the sun is in growing our gardens and we give them a little help by planting them in the right location. In the wild it's a constant battle to gain the sun's elusive light, a matter of life or death. Some trees like the mighty beeches, firs and spruces rise quickly to consume the daylight, leaving limited streams of light for the trees below. Their tall trunks absorb a good ninety-seven percent of the light and the forest floor is dark and void of color but still rich in nutrients. However, pools of light peek through the barren branches of the deciduous forests bringing to life a floor filled with a cascade of color.

The liverworts, a perennial in the buttercup family, take hold of the older forests in pink, purple and blue blooms. Butterflies, moths and bees are quite fond of their nectar. Blooms are short-lived from March to early May soaking in the sun while the deciduous trees are sleeping. In that short timeframe, they produce much-needed carbohydrates that will last them throughout the year. After the trees begin budding with leaves, the flowers begin their own hibernation for a good ten months.

But there are other plants that are tenacious in their ability to not only survive but cause problems for the masterful trees. Thin vines such as poison ivy and other ivy families are relentlessly climbing the tall trees eventually consuming the treetops. Like a mighty snake, they can squeeze the life out of trees.

The same style of strangulation takes place with another species that seems harmless in its lily-like flowers. The honeysuckle vine begins with the younger trees wrapping it so tightly around the trunks that it leaves a scar slowing its growth and weakening its trunk. Mistletoe wastes no time and instead of climbing they enlist the help of birds to deposit their sticky seeds in the upper branches. Once it's settled there, mistletoe begins to feast on the succulent wood. Depending on the number of plants and the amount of constant bloodletting, the parasite will eventually reduce the size of the tree's crown and the tree will eventually die.

However, the resurrection vines that transform from a lifeless brown to a vigorous green mean no harm. And the Spanish moss that eloquently hangs from the century-old oaks is another friend. They have no roots to sink into the soil or the branches, instead just small hair-like structures that feed on water from fog or rain. They do benefit from the oak's umbrella-like branches as the water funnels down the tree and the moss is there to collect the divine elixir.

WINTER, TIME TO REST

As Henry David Thoreau penned in his journal entry on October 29, 1858: "Nature now, like an athlete, begins to strip herself in earnest for her contest with her great antagonist Winter. In the bare trees and twigs what a display of muscle."

A cold winter helps protect trees as it kills pests and gives the tree a nice break like a long winter's nap. Scientists have also found that climate change has brought a disadvantage with certain species of trees. *The Hidden Life of Trees* notes that the warming of the cold season brings a deal of confusion for trees and plants. Especially in the south when trees begin to sprout leaves during warm spells in January, only to have them drop off at the next frost. Imagine what this is doing to the evolution of the tree's survival.

Some trees can even count, that is they can count the number of consecutive warm days. It is then they trust the season is changing. But beech trees take it one step further and actually wait until the days hold at least thirteen hours of daylight. So how do they do this?

Wohlleben believes a vital clue can be found in the leaves. Each leaf owns a type of solar cell that receives light waves to measure the length of daylight. Of course that can only be done in the summer. In spring, researchers surmise the buds own a similar tool. Wrapped around each leaf bud is a brown scale cover which helps protect the folded leaves from drying out. A closer look reveals the scale is transparent which helps the bud register the day length. Proof, says Wohlleben, that trees have a memory as they recognize rising temps by comparing day lengths and counting the warm days.

However, as temperatures continue to fluctuate due to climate change, more and more trees are befuddled in recognizing the change of seasons. Late spring frosts can cause a tree to lose valuable buds and leaves, while some trees take a gamble with warmer falls and hold onto their leaves all the way until November. In doing this the October storms can be more dangerous as the tree is heavier and cannot shed the wind.

❧ 3 ❧

CLIMATE CHANGE

Why is it trees get no respect? Why do so many ignore their velvet leaves and coarse branches? It is said that half the biomass in the forest is on the forest floor. Trees can live without the deer, wolves and carnivores, but they can't live without their vital soil. My bible on trees tells me there are more life forms in a handful of forest soil than there are people on the planet.

Remember, without soil, there would be no earth, which brings us back to the beginning, the dawn of time. The geological layers began with the ice age that eventually cracked open rocks and glaciers, then ground the stones into sand and dust. This material washed into depressions and valleys creating layers of soil. Inside the soil came bacteria, fungi and plants, which then began to form humus. Soon trees grew stabilizing the soil, slowing erosion and layers upon layers of humus packed the earth.

The forest is a gigantic carbon filled with an oxide that constantly filters and stores components. During its lifetime, a tree can filter the air by storing twenty-two tons of carbon dioxide. Even after its death, the organic remains of a tree continue to process it into a humus type substance.

Today's fossil fuels are in fact the remnants of trees that died 300 million years ago. Trees that died of old age, many six foot in diameter growing in the swamps that fell in the water but hardly rotted. Instead, after thousands of years, they turned into layers of thick peat, covered in rocky debris and the pressure gradually turned the peat into coal. Our cars and homes, along with power plants, are in essence burning fossil forests.

As Peter Wohlleben, so eloquently stated, "Wouldn't it be beautiful if we allowed our trees to follow in the footsteps of their ancestors by giving them the opportunity to recapture at least some of the carbon dioxide released by power plants and store it in the ground once again?"

With today's continued dissemination of trees, more and more of the protective humus layers are consumed by the sun which in turn releases more carbons in the atmosphere. As a result, these climate-changing gases equal the amount of timber that is felled.

So how do trees combat climate change? Or why do they bother? They, like humans, are a living community constantly fighting to survive and propagate. Although many trees have a built-in tolerance to adversity, they can only tolerate so much. When the climate becomes too warm, too cold, too dry or too wet the trees sense a change is in order and so they begin to migrate. They rely on the next generation; it is the trees embryo that is free to travel.

Tent Rocks New Mexico

Some species are quicker than others; it all depends on the composition of the seed. Those in a hurry produce offspring with fine hairs that are light as a feather and drift vicariously. Of course, they use a lot of energy in this long-distance travel, and these trees may be more susceptible to starvation and thirst. Trees with heavier seeds may not travel as far but are more equipped to survive. Some seeds are spread by birds and animals, a blue jay can send a seed miles and miles away while a squirrel can only manage a few hundred yards.

Wohlleben's book reminds us that we aren't helping matters by eliminating green space. Basically cutting back on our natural pollution purifier and what some even claim to be our fountain of youth.

Although there are techniques to gauge the age of a tree, there's no comparison of human years to the life of a tree. A thriving 120-year old tree compared to human years is barely out of high school. In fact a team of 100,000 scientists has found that the older the tree gets the more it grows, and so to fight climate change you must leave the forests alone and let them grow.

Trees are an industrious lot; after all, they are at the whims of Mother Nature. A tree funnels water during a generous rainstorm from the leaves and branches to the roots; a mature tree can accumulate and store hundreds of gallons of water for future dry spells. Which by the way is why so many urban landscapes are flooding, they have taken away their most efficient barrier of excess water.

These wooded wonders also transport water further inland, where clouds rising from oceans and rivers cannot reach. They do this through water vapor and transpiration, so much so it can create downpours a thousand miles inland. A coastal forest acts like a pump and if removed it can affect vast lands further inland. Evidence of this can be found in Brazil as the rainforest is drying out.

Even minute creatures are influenced by climate change. Wohlleben reminds us that forests nurse crucial organisms that feed snails, tadpoles and salamanders. Forests are like a sponge collecting rain along with filtering and managing stream water temperatures. The process of growing and losing leaves works hand in hand with the climate of the streams and the forest floor. Without the sun peeking through the bare branches of deciduous trees during the winter, the baby salamanders would die because the streams would freeze.

Evolution is the mainstay for survival in humans and smaller animals. Tress seem to live forever, ancient gods in the natural world, but then they live in a different dimension of time. It takes the young trees centuries rather than decades to even begin to mature and eventually propagate. This slow and methodical process doesn't do well with abrupt changes. So how do they adapt?

A telling example is laid out in *The Hidden Life of Trees*. Construction workers near Zürich came across what appeared to be fresh tree stumps. A curious researcher did some tests and discovered they were almost 14,000 years old during a period of major temperature fluctuations. It appeared the trees just stood still in time, like a time capsule waiting for the environment to become more adaptable.

Researchers have also found when the climate change is severe trees begin sending messages to their seeds just as they are ready to ripen. And as pointed out earlier trees have a memory, if they went through a recent severe drought they become more economical in disbursing moisture from the roots to the limbs. If the tree realizes that water continues to be in short supply it produces an extra layer of wax on the surface of its leaves. This helps keep the leaves watertight. More proof in a tree's amazing resilience to survive, that is as long as the forests are undisturbed by man.

GREATEST LOSS

Humboldt Redwoods State park, CA. Photo by Jason Sturner

Droves of visitors are drawn to parks throughout California to seek the beauty of sequoias and redwoods admiring that endearing contrast between the cinnamon-red bark and florescent green needles. Reaching up to the heavens, they seem invincible like mighty warriors refusing to bow down to the elements. But will they one day become an endangered species?

In an article on the LiveScience website we learn that these giants can live up to 3,500 years. Their main demise is root rot or some form of wearing of their base, but fire root rot and dry spells don't normally affect the entire tree. It is when the base becomes weak and gravity is the greatest enemy. With no foundation and due to their height, the tree falls. But it takes a long time, evident by their lifespan.

Increased droughts in California have scientists concerned says LiveScience, the trees gain most of their water from the Sierra Nevada snow, thousands of gallons every day. Scientists have witnessed many of the trees are stressed from lack of water, some have even died but still standing, while others suffering from dehydration with brown foliage at the top of the tree. One scientist noted in 2015 that it was the most stressed they have ever seen with giant sequoias.

The article went on to say that not all are suffering, Deborah Zierten, education and interpretation manager with the Save the Redwoods League noted that a giant sequoia's response to drought is dependent on location. What she believes is attributed to several factors including fire suppression, weather, location and amount of snowmelt exposure, and density of the trees.

Believe it or not one of the sequoias best friend is fire, but controlled fires. It helps remove the undergrowth which competes for water and is fuel for forest fires. Fire helps recycle nutrients and exposing bare soil which in turn helps the tree's new seedlings take root. The fire also eliminates lower trees allowing more sunlight for the young seedlings to grow. Many of the parks are beginning to ramp up the prescribed fires after suppressing them over the last several decades.

Meanwhile researchers are busy in understanding how climate change is affecting the trees. They admit the biggest and most immediate threat is lack of precipitation from the snow and increased wildfires.

COST OF CLIMATE CHANGE

Hurricane Katrina damage in southeast Louisiana

The seeds of this book began while researching the chapter Nature's Mystique in my 2016 release of *Spirits of the Bayou*. It was then I discovered the ancient language of trees. Although I've always felt connected to the forests and the creatures that live there, it opened a new world for me.

Determined to learn more, my continued research instilled a heightened awareness of the world around me, not only its inner beauty but also the menacing disruptions in today's climate.

Throughout this book are several mentions of Hurricane Katrina, both the history and personal experiences. As of November 1, just one month before the end of the 2017 Atlantic hurricane season, there have been fifteen named storms, ten hurricanes including six that reached a Category 3 or stronger.

The Weather Channel notes that the 2017 season continues to climb the ranks as one of most active seasons with the frantic stretch of destructive storms. A barometer in gauging the intensity of a season begins in looking back at the infamous 2004 and 2005 hurricane seasons. With one more month to go, currently the 2017 names storms equal the same number of storms in 2004, with an equal number of major hurricanes as noted by the Weather Channel.

The 2005 season shattered records reaching beyond the standard naming convention in letters of the alphabet with twenty eight tropical and subtropical storms. After Hurricane Wilma, the storms continued with names from the Greek Alphabet ending with Zeta. Fifteen of the storms reached hurricane strength and seven reached a Category 3 or stronger.

Although 2017 may not match the 2015 season, it's very close with six major hurricanes compared to the seven in 2015. There have also been four hurricanes that made a U.S. landfall in 2017, a first since twelve years ago in 2005 with six striking the U.S.

Multiple stories of despair and bravery were born in this active season. A NASA photo shares the fury and size of Hurricane Harvey. It dumped 51.88 inches of rain into Cedar Bayou, Texas, a record for rainfall in the continental U.S. according to the National Weather Service. All across the suburbs of Houston, Texas and Lake Charles, Louisiana, live helicopter rescues of people and animals filled the screens, that along with thousands walking in waist-deep waters.

Intense winds from Hurricane Irma and Maria wrecked havoc ripping through the Caribbean leaving nothing but rubble in its path. In a matter of hours, the Virgin Islands and Puerto Rico were unrecognizable, their tropical forests gone and with it no water, electricity or communication.

Even more frightening is watching it all unfold before our very eyes. Millions stayed glued to their televisions watching Irma crawl across the entire state of Florida and up through coastal and southern states dumping more rain and winds. Then came the fires in Santa Rosa and Sonoma County, California.

With the advent of high-tech media, we watch the angry flames devouring everything in its path. We read the heartbreaking stories of those who tried to escape inside residential swimming pools, some made it and others did not. The tears flow in a miraculous search of a dog, a pet that found his way back home. Stories of saving horses and farm animals in the path of the searing heat and flames. Another record-breaking natural disaster, the vineyards, the forests, and the lives lost, all victims of climate change.

The flames were fueled in part due the Diablo winds clocking in at seventy miles an hour, just five miles shy of hurricane force winds. Ironically it was the explosive combo of a wet winter and excessive summer heat that helped feed this record-breaking fire.

According to Inside Climate News, a Pulitzer Prize-winning, non-profit news organization, in an article written by reporter Georgina Gustin, a five-year drought left the forests very stressed and although the wet winter helped with the drought, the excessive water fed a huge crop of grasses and brush. The article went on to explain that with the state's hottest summer ever, all the grasses and vegetation dried up into massive acres of kindling.

The California fires took forty three lives and scorched 245,000 acres, destroyed or damaged 8,900 dwellings and displaced more than 100,000 people. A drone video of Santa Rosa shares a birds-eye view of torched neighborhoods, dropping lower it finds a sleek train moving slowly across the tracks. The train inches its way past the scorched rubble and smoldering trees, paying its respects for the families who lived there. Although the homes are gone, evidence can be found in a montage of lonely chimneys, melted trampolines and charred swing sets.

In 2017 California has already experienced a record 11,200 fires. The article noted that although 2017 may not pass the country's 2015 record of ten million acres burned, the amount of money the government has spent in fighting fires has reached an all-time high at two billion dollars.

Another article in the same publication reported by Sabrina Shankman shares some alarming statistics in the cost of climate change. The combined devastation of Harvey, Irma, Maria and the dozens of wildfires is reaching what could be the costliest string of weather events in U.S. history. Based on a report released by a nonprofit Universal Ecological Fund, the damage is near $300 billion dollars. And that's just in 2017.

There's obviously a trend here, one that cannot be ignored not only because of the horrific damage but the rising cost. One of the authors of the report, Robert Watson, cited that the growing numbers of extreme weather events are a continuation of a three-decades trend with increased storms, hurricanes, flooding, droughts and wildfires.

He continued to explain that the more fossil fuels we burn, the faster the climate changes. The country and the world must work together to build a low-carbon economy in order to maintain a positive economic growth.

Currently, the United States is more in a reactionary mode with a price tag averaging $240 billion each year over the last decade. The report estimated that future costs could easily reach $360 billion annually. Which isn't far from what U.S. has spent thus far in 2017. And that's only the rescue dollars, the restoration expense will continue to mount for years to come.

In August 2016 it was catastrophic flooding from a rain event in the state of Louisiana, not coastal flooding or a raging hurricane. Throughout parishes (counties) surrounding the capital of Baton Rouge, thirty inches of rain damaged or destroyed more than 50,000 homes, 100,000 vehicles and 20,000 businesses. The saddest part was seventy-five million had no flood insurance because they were not in a flood-prone region. That price tag was ten-billion dollars and many more states are experiencing the same record-breaking weather events.

A New Orleans park turns into a wasteland of debris from Hurricane Katrina

Seems pretty obvious that we are in need of a more dedicated solution. A global commitment to be more energy efficient and reduce greenhouse gases, but there are increasing naysayers fueled by political factions. In reading the 2017 headlines of a new administration, it seems the country is going backward, ignoring the warnings and removing the restrictions on coal and carbon gas pollutants. Perhaps money speaks louder than words, in this case, the rising billions spent on repairing the damage.

Perhaps it's time to go back, back to the generations before us, before the industrial revolution when we revered nature. When we were partners with the land around us, working together and only taking what we could sow.

NATURAL SOLUTIONS

Central Louisiana dairy pasture

In 2015, 195 nations came together in Paris to negotiate a strategic plan to address climate change. Known as the Paris Agreement, the international leaders established the United Nation's seventeen Sustainable Development Goals, which included to fight poverty, promote sustainability and address climate change. Soon after, two hundred countries came together in Paris pledging their commitment to the world's largest international climate treaty. Their goal is to reach net zero greenhouse gas emissions by mid-century to restrict the global temperature to stay under 2° C.

It's an industrious endeavor but one the international community is ready to address, to protect the earth's delicate ecosystems and to stop those who are monopolizing the planet's resources for profit.

In fact, it seems Mother Nature is sounding the alarm loud and clear, she's flexing her muscles with the increased climatological catastrophes around the world. She's sending a message that it's bad business to ignore the signs, or for some, even ignore the existence of climate change as the price tag for disaster relief continues to grow.

In an October 2017 report published in the Proceedings of the National Academy of Sciences, The Nature Conservancy and fifteen other institutions brought forth data and evidence that the powers of nature are a critical factor in managing climate change. Granted it sounds overly simplistic, but now we have science to prove the obvious.

The findings show that these nature-based solutions can reduce emissions by thirty-seven-percent by 2030, what is said to be thirty-percent more than previously thought. Studying landscapes around the world and examining nature's mitigation potential could mean a reduction of slightly more than eleven billion tons of emissions or the equivalent of eliminating the burning of oil across the globe.

While most countries are concentrating on reducing fossil fuel emission, the Nature Conservancy report stresses natural climate solutions such as conservation, restoration and better management of forests, grasslands and wetlands. Part of the research involved measuring the carbon impact of logging in old growth forests, along with varying efficiencies of different forest ecosystems in absorbing and storing carbon from the atmosphere.

Bronson Griscom, Director of Forest Carbon Science at the Nature Conservancy found that forest loss accounts for eight to ten percent of global carbon emissions. The Amazon rainforests is one of the largest in filtering massive amounts of carbon.

Griscom reported one region that has gotten less attention from climate regulators is managed land such as farmlands, peatlands, seagrass and tidal marshes. A large team of scientists from fifteen research institutions began to investigate, do a little number crunching in the potential of these landscapes in reducing carbon emissions. It became the most comprehensive study on the role nature can play in meeting the Paris Climate agreement.

The report conceded that based on the current timeline in reducing fossil fuel emissions, the Paris Agreement is falling short with an estimated temperature of 4°C. Based on that summation, and the fact we can't afford to wait, scientists got to work in looking for natural solutions, after all nature has been reducing carbon dioxide for hundreds of millions of years.

Clean energy technologies such as recycling, renewables, electric cars and energy efficiency products are admirable, and continued growth in those commodities are showing progress, but there needs to be equal commitment to investments in natural solutions as well. Windmills are another piece of the cost effective grid that benefits many communities.

Griscom's natural climate solutions are broken down by forests, wetlands, agricultural lands and grasslands, which are then broken into a taxonomy of twenty specific pathways to fully utilize nature's potential. Different practices are noted including the low-cost opportunities, and extended benefits such as water filtration, flood buffering, improved soil health, protection of biodiversity habitat, and enhanced climate resilience.

If these practices are mobilized over the next ten to fifteen years, the report noted that thirty-seven-percent of the needed mitigation will be accomplished. However, if it's delayed until after 2030, the number drops to thirty-three percent and continues to drop with every advancing decade.

Like many countries, forest loss due to capital gain is an every-increasing dilemma. Case in point is Indonesia, a country that owns the world's third largest tropical rainforest but has also been hit with the most deforestation. The Nature Conservancy report notes the rapid decline of the forest ecosystems account for nearly fifty-percent of the country's emissions. But like most countries across the globe, it's difficult to balance economic growth with sustainable development.

The Natural Climate Solutions findings offer a starting point, a guide for cost-effective implantation of their twenty natural pathways. Broken down in savings, the forest pathways account for nearly half of the lowest-cost climate endeavors, while the grassland stands at a quarter and the wetlands is nearly a fifth. Of course it depends on the country and specific locale, the scales could swing in different proportions.

Wetlands offer a natural barrier against monster storms for coastal states and larger inland cities. Today, the price tag continues to rise when repeated tropical storms and hurricanes eat away their coastline.

Cypress forest along the Louisiana coast, another victim of
coastal erosion

Louisiana for example has been fighting coastal erosion of their
wetlands for decades. They are losing valuable coastlines with saltwater intrusion based on rising water levels and small canals dug by
the oil companies. They have lost livelihoods, homes and entire
towns, even historical properties once owned by local Indian tribes.
Many residents find themselves having to move further inland in order
to stay ahead of the encroaching water.

As Bronson Griscom reminded everyone in a quote posted on The
Natural Conservancy website, "Biodiversity loss in the wetlands and
rainforests, nutrient-rich soil issues for farmers, indigenous people's
forest rights...it's all connected."

And the larger the trees, the more vital they are in reducing carbon
emissions. Redwoods are a gift and they have graced this planet with
their presence for more than 240 million years.

Both the redwoods and sequoias play an important role in miti-
gating climate change according to Deborah Zierten with the Save The
Redwoods League. Provided the trees are so huge, they can take in
more dangerous carbon, a natural filter and storage unit. Noted in a
Redwoods and Climate Change Initiative study, "Ancient redwood
forests store at least three times more carbon above ground than any
other forests on Earth."

Photo by Tony Webster, Lady Bird Johnson Grove, Redwood State Park, CA

Another vital element is the age of the trees, they are ancient or at the very lest old-growth forests and so they can retain these carbons for a very long time. Zierten emphasized it's the entire forest, live and dead because even fallen trees store carbon as do the under-story plants.

She recommends we do more to keep our older forests healthy. Besides the prescribed burning, the Save the Redwoods League restores creeks and helps remove many of the roads built during the logging booms which causes erosion. And of course the more the public visits the parks, the more engaged they will be to keep these forests alive for future generations.

4

FATE OF THE FOREST

New Orleans City Park

We all long for that Holy Grail moment, sitting under our favorite tree wasting away the day or walking through the jungle of Muir Woods, our heart ticking like a Joni Mitchell ballad, or perhaps it's just getting our hands dirty working in the garden breathing in that earthy aroma.

I believe there is a spiritual brotherhood between the wild and the lovers of the same. And Annie Dillard, author of the book *Pilgrim At Tinker Creek* shares similar values. I've read this book twice and now on my third reading, it's that kind of book. On a trip through the Blue Ridge Parkway in the fall of 2015, I felt compelled to take a back road, it was our last day there. My husband drove past a sign that said Tinker Creek, yes Annie's Tinker Creek. There we were 855 miles from home inside a cathedral of trees blazing with fiery colors, what were the odds?

Time didn't allow a stop, that perennial curse we all share, that almighty clock with no regard to the everlasting beauty of holy grounds. Dillard lives on Tinker Creek in what she calls an anchorite's hermitage, an anchor she says that keeps her there. Her creek, like nature itself is a mystery, a continuous creation and all it shares, in what she proclaims in her book, "…the uncertainty of vision, the horror of the fixed, the dissolution of the present, the intricacy of beauty, the pressure of fecundity, the elusiveness of the free, and the flawed nature of perfection."

I too have a creek, more narrow, more riparian than the rocky confines of Tinker Creek, but home to great blue herons and the like. It too has an anchor, a spell that holds me hostage, one I welcome with all its beauty and its woe. There in the woods, I work in what I call my outside office. Pounding on the keys I'm invigorated by the sparrow's repeated calls echoing across the trees.

Surrounded by books, books on trees, nature's healing, Thoreau quotes and of course Dillard's book. Getting lost in the pages of nature's wonders, a tiny insect crawls across the sentences like hiking through a forest. Another flies on my computer screen curious to see what all the fuss is about. Curious, or maybe, just maybe, they are welcoming me to their home. But there are times when I feel the forests are restless, perhaps they are echoing my own fear, or maybe they hear what I hear.

In the distance there are sounds of developers fighting to win the battle, to conquer and consume the land. Backhoes and bulldozers march through the forests while the critters panic trying to gather their young, squirrels scurry to find cover while deer race across busy highways. The greedy developers explain it is cheaper to level a forest than to spare a strand of trees. We'll plant new ones they tell the city council, and all is well with the world. Do they honestly think a forest can be replaced with a couple of spindly trees that never get watered? Of course not, nor do they care.

And then the floods come because the water has nowhere to go as the concrete acts as a horizontal dike. Often times the strip shopping malls and gas stations are built on wetlands and the developers bring in loads of dirt to fill the property. After the heavy rains, the water finds its lowest point, which is usually residential neighborhoods.

To think it could all be prevented if they just left the trees alone. One of my favorite parks is the New Orleans City Park, which I share in a later chapter. Their website reminds us how important it is to protect our trees as they are the first line of defense with flooding rains and storms. A mature bald cypress can absorb as much as 880 gallons of water in one day, now imagine, a forest filled with cypress trees.

For now, my piece of paradise is safe, a sweet concert of sounds, the bird's flute-like chirps, the frog's throaty melody and the moving symphony of the cicadas. Dillard shares my infatuation with the sounds of the forest and the miracles that they bring. Her book details the life of cicadas, they have a breeding cycle of thirteen years, adults lay the eggs in slits along the twig bark then the hatched nymphs fall to the ground burrowing deep into the earth.

There in the dark and damp confines of tree roots, they ramble for thirteen long years never seeing the light of day. April is the month of reckoning when the nymphs crawl from their thirteen-year dank home, digging their way to the surface inching up trees and shrubs shedding their skins. It is then they bless us with the sweet song of spring, what Dillard prescribes as that hollow, shrill grind with a plaintive, mysterious urgency that lasts all summer.

Cypress knees on forest floor

Retreating to my upstairs office I feel connected to the trees, their thick branches right outside my window filled with busy squirrels and a front-row seat to warblers feasting along the branches. The sun splashes across the trees and I watch the graceful dance of the pines swaying to the beat of the hearty breezes. Suddenly a small humming-bird spies me through the window. He swings by close and stares at me, his wings moving in a constant blur, he is summing me to fill his feeder. It's not the first time this has happened, could it be we are all connected, all creatures of the woods? I believe it to be true.

As I type this blissful message I turn to Henry David Thoreau searching for an answer and find his August 17, 1851, journal entry:

"The cricket, the gurgling stream, the rushing wind amid the trees, all speak to me soberly yet encouragingly of the steady onward progress of universe. My heart leaps into my mouth at the sound of the wind in the woods. I whose life was but yesterday so desultory and shallow suddenly recovering through the still, louring day, and am reminded of the peeping flocks which will soon herald the thoughtful season. Ah! If I could so live that there should be no desultory moment in all my life!"

Some say trees incorporate a complete biosystem. That is they carefully keep their energies levels in proper proportions. And although we know they rely on a community of trees for assistance, each tree still must find a way to feed and defend itself. Most of the tree's energy is used for daily living, to breath, digest its food, supply its fungal allies with sugar and grow a little bit every day. And then they always keep a hidden reserve to fight off those pesky pests.

Much research has been done in examining the secret reserves, like their own personal disinfectant that can create a germ-free force field. *The Hidden Life of Trees* shares research from Boris Tokin, a biologist from Leningrad. His paper revealed that when crushed spruce and pine needles are placed in a cup of water filled with protozoa, the protozoa are dead in a matter of seconds. And the air in young pine forests is almost germ-free. In fact walking among these pristine giants can boost your immune system. In essence, each tree works hard in maintaining a healthy environment for itself and for both the natural and human community.

Growing urban populations are increasingly consuming rural land-scapes, often times clearing trees and forests. The increased consumption of food, energy and water, brings more civil and commercial developments. It doesn't take long to see the polluted urban environment begin to affect the health and quality of life.

Developers decimate forests building ghost-town style subdivisions with their perfectly manicured lawns. Soon begins a spiraling degradation of the environment. Homeowners move in and build outdoor patios and pools that consume their yard. Then the entertaining begins with complaints there are too many mosquitoes. The government comes to their rescue and douses the skies, homes and the people with insecticides. Trucks roll down the streets spewing a deadly fog across ground-level grasses while the airplanes zoom across the rooftops dropping loads of poison across the trees and nearby forests.

I have witnessed the degradation over the last three decades living here in my wooded kingdom. The lightning bugs (fireflies) are gone, the butterflies a bare minimum and a decrease in animals. Even the forests are becoming a ghost town.

With a little research, it's easy to manage pest control with plants that have natural compounds that are far more effective against insects. Smart garden lovers should plant walnut trees on their property as they emit a heady scent that is even more intense on hot summer days; it is this natural force field that keeps the mosquitoes away.

And so the greatest and cruelest enemy of trees is man. It begins in the nursery, a term humans think of fondly as a caring and loving environment. Instead, it is the beginning of torture for the defenseless trees. The roots are routinely trimmed to restrict the tree's size until they leave the nursery. In doing so they are causing great pain to the tree amputating the tree's brains found along the sensitive tips of each root.

Once planted the poor trees lose their sense of direction and confused when searching for water and food. They find themselves in a foreign land surrounded by concrete and their roots have nowhere to go. Unlike the porous floor of the old growth forest, the stunted roots find it difficult to travel through heavily trampled soil.

Healthy trees that live in the forest limit their roots to five-foot deep because they have the advantage of sending their roots far and wide. Their roots mingle with other trees and nourished by the community of life. Without a proper foundation, the urban trees become top heavy and susceptible to damaging storms.

Urban trees are adeptly titled Street Kids by *The Hidden Life of Trees* book and restricted by underground pipes and dense soil compacted by heavy machinery. Some trees in a desperate attempt to survive send their roots horizontally looking for a more amicable environment. It is there they find the underground wastewater pipes and are attracted to the loose soil that surrounds them. This bold attempt to survive in fact leads to their death.

Once the city determines the guilty party, the tree is executed and thrown into a landfill with rotting food. Ironically another tree is placed in the same spot but this time caged like a prisoner forbidding it to continue such a valiant behavior.

Even more disgraceful is when local governments declare their affection for the environment imposing strict guidelines for developers. Zoning rules state they must plant a required number of trees based on the number of acres they clear. However, they plant tiny saplings often struggling for water, and their dedication to giving back to the environment ends there. Even if some of these trees should survive they cannot bear the grueling temperatures. The urban microclimate is surrounded by asphalt and concrete that holds the heat. Unlike the forest that cools itself on those hot summer nights, that radiant heat stays long after the sun sets and full of exhaust fumes which makes the tree easy prey for pests.

To make matters worse they are drowned with fertilizers, blistered by daily dog walks, and winter salts do similar damage. These painful injuries are often revealed in a mix of yellow and brown spots that appear on leaves and needles. Some are mutilated experiencing great pain from excessive pruning so every tree is the same size or to clear enough room for pedestrians. Trees die prematurely losing their battle in fighting these so-called caregivers.

Do these manufactured urban trees know their native language, or has that been silenced as well? Do they know what it is like to be free, to spread their roots in a new land?

The demise of our green space is my overarching fear, the demon that never rests. Perhaps what's even more sad is that generations of tree huggers, even Druids have repeatedly tried their best in educating those who are blind to the intricate web between our forests and mankind. We have made great strides in reducing animal abuse, and many have removed meat from their diet. And although most do believe trees are a living entity, Wohlleben signs off in his last chapter proclaiming although many may see trees as a living being, most still see them as a commodity.

"We should care about them because of the little puzzles and wonders they present us with. Under the canopy of the trees, daily dramas and moving love stories are played out. Here is the last remaining piece of Nature, right on our doorstep, where adventures are to be experienced and secrets discovered."

Creatives across the world continue to pen their protests and script the beauty of the wild, advocates for these silent giants. Even Thoreau in his early 20s pondered the demise equating the decimation of the forests with the slaughter of the whale for its oil and the elephant for its ivory. He questions who is the lover of the trees; is it the lumberman?

Thoreau proclaims in the early 1800s:

"No! no! It is the poet; it is he who make the truest use of the pine, who does not fondle it with an axe, nor tickle it with a saw, nor stroke it with a plane, who knows where its heart is false without cutting into it, who has not bought the stumpage of the township on which it stands. All the pines shudder and heave a sigh when that man steps on the forest floor. No, it is the poet, who loves them as is own shadow in the air, and lets them stand. It is the spirit of the tree, not its spirit of the turpentine, with which I sympathize, and which heals my cuts. It is as immortal as I am, and perchance will go to as high a heaven, there to tower above me still."

NATURE'S CURE

Humans have become too cloistered, wired to their electronics and prisoners of everyday life. We have become disconnected to the very thing that gave us life, the animalistic desire to live in the wild. The romantics begged us to listen, poets, writers, artists and musicians penning their prose desperate to save our creative soul. Instead, we consumed mass quantities of pills to relieve the pain when the answer was in our own backyard, our local parks, and most of all our trees.

Trees provide healing anecdotes, a tonic for humans, an escape, a cure for what the book, *The Nature Fix*, called "nature deficit disorder." Author Florence Williams, a journalist, left her cozy mountain woods of Boulder, Colorado to Washington, D.C., and immediately felt the disorder.

It isn't until recently that scientists the world over have begun their own research. How often have I complained of the same malaise? I have endured incredulous heat and cold while working in what I call my outside office.

Williams not only toured foreign countries in search of answers but shadowed many researchers in the U.S. to prove her hypothesis.

Photo by Roman Boed, a stream in the German Black Forest near Baiersbronn

Scientists have come together trying to unlock the miracles of nature, its medicinal attributes from better memory to adding years to your life. In Japan, they have coined it the biophilia hypothesis working hard to prove nature lowers stress and boosts mental health. Williams believes we feel more at home inside nature because that's where we evolved. A neuroscientist at the University of Utah prescribes at least a five-hour dose of nature every month.

Perhaps one of the most telling statistics was when the World Health Organization officially declared we became an urban species in 2008 after the majority of the worldwide population became city dwellers. Be it for better or for worse, it is the first time in the history of mankind that there are more people living in urban areas versus rural. And in the U.S., cities grew faster than suburbia for the first time in a hundred years.

Could there be a correlation between the increased urban population to higher crime and behavioral problems? The book, *The Nature's Fix*, shared an experiment in a Chicago housing project where academic researchers selected 145 single mothers and randomly placed them in apartments with different views. They found the residents staring into an asphalt wasteland reported higher levels of physiological aggression compared to those who lived in apartments gazing into courtyards filled with trees and green space.

For a more objective conclusion, the same researchers turned to the police reports analyzing ninety-eight buildings over two years. The book shares a stunning result with increased numbers of assaults, homicides, vehicle thefts, burglary and arson with those who lived in concrete courtyards versus those who enjoyed lush landscapes.

Families privileged with landscaped courtyards experienced a forty-eight percent reduction in property crimes and fifty-six percent fewer violent crimes. The appealing courtyards brought the community together, neighbors were more social and looked out for each other.

But what is the core reason humans are attracted to nature? Could it be some deep-seeded need to return to the wild? Perhaps we just long for old-fashioned romanticism, but now there's science to prove our hypothesis.

OUR LOVE OF GREEN

Bayou Benoit in Louisiana's Atchafalaya Basin

Driving down a long highway nestled between thick canopies of forests, there's that familiar deep green set against a wide-open sky. A sky so blue at times you feel like you're flying through the air into the heavens. What is it about that vibrant green and cobalt colored sky that gives us so much energy, a love beyond words?

What we see is a relaxing portrait, but for the trees, it means working overtime. Yes, they do like light and rays of sun pouring down across their leaves, but blue for a tree is quite tedious.

However you could say that the tree is playing a trick on us, it seems the color green isn't really green. In his book, Peter Wohlleben reminds us that chlorophyll helps leaves process light, but the trees don't use all of the chlorophyll, what's referred to as the "green gap." Because it cannot use that part of the color spectrum, it reflects it back as unused. And we see this leftover as a deep green. How ironic that what we see as the trees real beauty, is in fact, part of a useless component.

Have you ever noticed the green light that falls gently across the forest, that mystical light that gives us peace? That's the leftover the trees don't use. Which begs another question, have we become numb to the beauty? Today's world is so dependent on fast moving flashy colors; it's a wonder that more and more have little time or patience for the beauty of trees and forests.

Even though at times it looks like a boring blur of green, it is home to millions of species, although many are hidden. The darker the forest, the more empty it seems. Perhaps it's because our mind and sight are conditioned to only see the obvious, the larger species. Instead, it is here in the deep forests where the plants thrive, where the butterflies mingle in earth-tone colors blending with the barks of trees. They are all natives of these ancient forests, a community that thrives on each other.

To better understand the science of our affection for nature's colors, Florence Williams interviewed Richard Taylor, a physicist, a nanoparticle physicist. It seems Taylor became enthralled in a decades-long research project studying the intricate works of the famed artist, Jackson Pollock.

Taylor was mesmerized by Pollock's abstract expressionism style of art. But there's more. Taylor is also an artist, a painter and photographer with two art degrees. Like most curious scientists, Taylor sought to find the answer in what drove Pollock and his style of work.

In Pollock's painting Autumn Rhythm, the complexity of his talent shines through in repeated layers of color and density. On display at the New York Met (Metropolitan Museum), their website shares Pollock's primeval flair as a complex web of white, brown and turquoise lines which bring a deeper dimension giving the piece visual rhythms and sensations.

His style of drip painting delivers opposing textures: light and dark, thick and thin, heavy and buoyant, and straight and curved. Multi-dimensional layers captivate the viewer, what the Met describes, "Autumn Rhythm is evocative of nature, not only in its title but also in its coloring, horizontal orientation and sense of ground and space."

Taylor was so obsessed by Pollock's work he built a free-flowing pendulum that splattered paint when the wind blew. He wanted to see how nature would paint a picture. And the result was quite compelling, the "nature" painting mimicked Pollock's work.

Continuing his work as a physicist Taylor was assigned the task to find the most efficient way to move electricity. He discovered the movements of the currents of electricity were fractal, they repeat at different scales. In studying these fractal patterns, Taylor realized it reminded him of Pollock's poured paintings.

As the book notes, the paint splatters across the canvas like the flow of electricity, and so Taylor surmised that Pollock's paintings resembled nature's fractals. In fact, it was soon learned that Pollock's patterns are similar to trees, snowflakes and mineral veins.

Forested trails in Prince William County, VA

The patterns are found in varying degrees of nature, from the clouds, leaves, coastlines, ocean waves to clusters in the galaxies. When gazing at a tree, the human eye focuses on varying textures of the tree trunk, the branches that extend outward and even the minute veins on each leaf. We basically see the beauty all at once rather than a chaotic cluster of nature's work.

So again, what does all this prove? It seems scientists and mathematicians have mind-boggling equations to prove these fractal patterns.

Taylor and an environmental psychologist conducted various experiments measuring brain activity when people were exposed to nature photos of landscapes turned into fractal silhouettes. The book notes scientists found people respond the most when exposed to the 1.3 and 1.5 fractal range, what they call the magic zone.

Based on these findings they also found that individuals could experience the same effect with similar patterns on a wall or working in an office with a window. Continuing medical research hopes to use this fractal data to help restore brain damage for stroke victims.

Okay so now we can definitely say that there's scientific proof that humans are drawn to nature due to its calming effect. In fact, this visual system has shown stress is reduced when the fractal structure of the eye matches the fractal image being viewed. Research revealed that the movement of the eye's retina owns the same fractal elements of nature. Scientists also found that our pupils use a search pattern that is fractal scanning the larger picture and then transfers it into smaller versions.

Basically, this does answer the initial question, "Are we attracted to nature in a deep-seeded need to return to the wild?" Perhaps it's a piece of DNA that is buried deep inside all humans, one that remains today as researchers have found it's a critical task in utilizing these fractal equations to quickly assess a scene.

Of course, it's not to say that we don't endear the Arcadian romance of nature, it's more in how we get there and that we need more of it. As we continue to build concrete temples and sky-high office buildings, we nullify our natural-stress reducers, that visual fluency.

Perhaps we can develop artificial fractal elements, architects integrate them in various works. I for one am not a proponent of this Orwellian future, if anything, add potted plants in offices and terrariums in office buildings. And forget about those 3D-virtual escapes that launch you into foreign lands with rainbow waterfalls or lying on a beach without fear of sunburn or skin cancer.

Software developers are studying the same research, measuring which colors are more pleasurable to the eye. Working hard in developing more enticing nature scenes, and most likely used in commercials as well.

Humans own three color cones in their retinas that pick up red, blue and green, and these cone cells speak directly to the brain's visual cortex. Most mammals only have two, while butterflies have five. Red excites while blue, green and pink are soothing, perhaps it's because these are the colors of nature.

But we must be careful in how we ingest color. Continued use of computer screens, phones, and virtual eyewear has increased cases of myopia (nearsightedness), especially in teens. Sunlight stimulates the release of dopamine, which helps prevent the eyeball from growing too oblong. Seems like a simple solution would be reading a print book outside under the shade of your favorite tree.

NATURE'S CURE FOR CHILDREN

Rocky Mountain National Park

Poets, writers and photographers have preached the gospel of nature for generations. From the sounds of a stream trickling down a mountain to the simple chatter of songbirds whistling in the wind.

Amazing how quickly many have lost that lust for nature. The adventures of childhood, building forts in the woods and playing outside from dawn to dusk has evaporated in just one generation. Be it the move to more urban surroundings or the lack of parks, it seems children spend their time trying to juggle multiple club meetings and band practices.

Indeed nature is the cure for many human ailments, both body, and mind. An engaging find in the book, *The Nature Fix* tackles newfound behavioral challenges such as ADHD (attention-deficit hyperactivity disorder). Many attribute ADHD to an increased number of children being cloistered playing video games and constant television viewing. With little or no exercise, some have become a type of attention mutant in school.

The medical industry immediately begins prescribing medications at an early age. Some schools even force parents to participate in this madness which many times offers little relief.

Could it be the world, or at least, many of American schools prefer rigid behaviors? Stay in your seat, don't talk back, and even recess, if it hasn't been eliminated, owns an equal amount of restrictions. Children learn from exploration, being challenged, learn how to cross a creek, climb a tree, or something so rudimentary as identifying poison ivy leaves.

Humans have evolved by taking chances and exploring beyond their capabilities. Some of us don't always follow the herd. For centuries there were those brave souls that lead the way into uncharted territory.

Those wilderness iconoclasts like John Muir, the hero of America's national parks, who as a child, scaled seaside cliffs in Dunbar, Scotland. Another American hero, Mark Twain left school at the age of twelve and embarked on life-long adventures down the Mississippi River and across the world. Ansel Adams was another unruly child; his parents pulled him out of school and gave him a Brownie camera. The family took off to tour Yosemite and the rest is history.

Even people like Thomas Edison who suffered from the same symptoms of ADHD was granted more than a thousand patents including the invention of the light bulb and the phonograph. The youngest of seven children, he was what the teachers called a hyperactive child prone to distractions and deemed too difficult for school. His mother, a schoolteacher, pulled him from school and taught him at home. At the age of eleven, he had a voracious appetite for knowledge on a wide range of subjects.

According to the biography website, he began working at twelve selling newspapers to passengers along the Grand Trunk Railroad in Michigan and later began publishing his own small newspaper. Besides an inventor, he was a master at developing businesses and spent most of his time reading and experimenting. He continued working until the age of 84 and died of complications of diabetes in October 1931.

And so is the story of many teens in today's society, misfits of sorts that don't fit in the same mold as others. But could it be they just have more active imaginations, a drive to learn more, a thirst for knowledge beyond the textbook? *The Nature Fix* book shares an enlightening story in how teens that have been labeled an outcast have found a new camaraderie in the wild outdoors. After all, if nature is a healing utopia for adults, why not children and teenagers?

Enchanted Rock Park in Fredericksburg Texas

According to the book, there's been promising progress with adventure-based boarding schools for grades seven through twelve. They are costly, comparative to upscale boarding schools, but show amazing results for those suffering from ADHD. One school mentioned was the Academy at SOAR. Teenagers that once had the attention of a gnat changed their attitudes and social skills after camping out and scaling rock in Wyoming.

There's still classroom time but you won't find ceiling-high walls filled with books. The school is accredited and does include the necessary academics, but history is discussed on site in the middle of a battlefield, and a geology lecture while camping and exploring on land more than 45 million years old.

Going back to the basics of climbing, backpacking and canoeing are the perfect anecdotes for kids in these age groups. What the book notes is a time when their neurons are exploding in a million different directions with an opportunity to find new ways of solving problems. Scientists believe it could be the perfect recharge for the prefrontal cortex allowing for a better attention span.

Teens with ADHD have different chemistry in the part of the brain that governs reward, movement and attention. They are easily bored and always on the lookout for activity that floods their brains with the feel-good neurotransmitters like dopamine, serotonin and norepinephrine.

Research shows that a dynamic outdoor learning environment is far more beneficial than our traditional schools packed with cloistered corridors. And it needs to happen sooner than later.

Childhood illnesses have increased since the seismic shift to stay indoors. Believe it or not, the fastest growing market for antidepressants in the U.S. are preschoolers. More than ten thousand American preschoolers are being medicated for ADHD. *The Nature Fix* book reported that the suicide rate has increased including a two hundred percent rise among girls ten to fourteen years old.

The obesity rates have tripled, the allergy and asthma rates are drastically climbing, as well as vitamin D deficiency. It is said that 76 million children are vitamin D insufficient due to lack of sunlight, which also helps regulate sleep. The vitamin is also responsible for bone growth and boosting immunity.

So where do we begin, not everyone can afford the privilege of these high priced outdoor schools. It begins at home and in the schools. Parents need to put more pressure on their children's schools, demand more time for recess, more outside curriculums.

We all need to ration the use of phones and video games, and connect more kids to nature. Inner city complexes and schools need more green space as well as school gardens so they can teach their families how to grow food. We can't afford to numb these children and destroy their neurons. We can't afford to lose the next John Muir, Ansel Adams and Mark Twain.

PLANT MORE TREES

According to the New Orleans City Park website, a mature tree absorbs 120 to 240 pounds of pollutants every year, while an average, healthy tree can produce 260 pounds of oxygen annually. Even more amazing is that two trees can supply enough oxygen for one person per year. The site pressed on encouraging Americans to plant trees, if every American planted just one tree, we could reduce the amount of carbon dioxide in the atmosphere by one billion pounds annually. Compared to nearly five percent that humans pump into the air every year, we would be well on our way to winning the battle on pollution.

In closing her book, Florence Williams shared some alarming statistics. It's obvious more and more urban trees are being decimated, green space in Washington D.C. has decreased to a canopy of only thirty-six percent, a decrease from fifty percent in 1950.

Health benefits, both physical and mental, have been repeated several times in the course of writing this book. There are always the naysayers, but the hard-core evidence is making its mark. Williams notes what she calls an astounding study by Geoffrey Donovan, an urban forester with the U.S. Forest Service. Published in 2013, it shares how a destructive insect, the emerald ash borer, decimated one hundred million ash trees throughout the Midwest and Northeast. At the same time of the annihilation, there was an increase of cardiovascular disease in humans.

Donovan recalled multiple studies across the world that shared similar links between the loss of green space and human stress and illness. One in Scotland even showed lower mortality rates near urban parks.

In examining the counties that were hit the hardest with the ash tree loss, Donovan noted there were fifteen thousand additional deaths due to cardiovascular disease and six thousand more from respiratory disease. That's an increase of ten percent, but why? Could it be the air quality dropped with the loss of "green" filtration or that there was more stress without the soothing nature of trees? Either way, it's enough to make urban planners take notice.

Toronto agrees and has invested in the health of its citizens to the tune of a seven billion dollar urban forest. They took notice in a recent study that showed the higher the neighborhood's tree density, the lower incident of heart and metabolic disease. When you break down the economic factor, it benefits both the residents and the city of Toronto as both invest in a government-run health care system.

Cities across America are taking notice. Washington, D.C. is working with nonprofits to plant at least eighty-six hundred trees a year to increase the tree canopy to forty percent in twenty years. New York City hopes to plant one million trees along with similar projects in Los Angeles and Denver.

Imagine if you told a politician or civil engineer how they could cut costs with a product that owns little or no overhead. Data from one report found that adding more trees could save megacities as much as $1.2 million per square mile or $35 a resident per year. It's basically free ecosystems with a positive return.

Let's hope this book and many others like it will bring a deeper awareness to the critical nature of our environment. We need to invest more resources into capital conservation and curtail development exploitation; to build an enriched society and economic stability. Washington, D. C. is well known for their trail of cherry trees and a popular jogging trail for many of the city's employees.

THE GREEN CURE

German forester and author of *The Hidden Life of Trees*, Peter Wohlleben agrees forests offer a medicinal vacation. Trees are natural air filters, particularly when you are strolling under them. As the wind floats through leaves and needles, the trees catch large and small particles, up to 20,000 tons of material per year per square mile. Coniferous forests actually help those who suffer from allergies.

Some believe trees can talk but how often do we listen? A case in point Wohlleben shared in his book, Korean scientists began testing older women as they walked through forests and urban areas. The women's blood pressure, lung capacity, and the electricity of their arteries improved when strolling through the trees, but their excursion into town showed none of these changes. An argument could be made this is an example of tree chatter, of course in a language all their own.

Wohlleben confessed that walkers who visit some of the ancient deciduous preserves that he manages always report their heart feels lighter and they feel right at home. But if they walk inside the more fragile/artificial coniferous forests in Central Europe, they don't feel the same. And so he concludes that perhaps our brains do receive the language of trees as the healthy forests convey more contented messages. Rather than hear the message, we breathe in their contentment that is then translated by our brains.

He continues to explain that every walk in the forest is like taking a shower of oxygen. Trees breathe through their long slender needles with narrow slips on the underside that look like a tiny mouth. They use these openings to exhale oxygen and breathe in carbon dioxide. Trees also breathe through their roots especially when they lose their leaves during the winter.

Finland is proud of their tree-hugging clan where ninety-five percent of their population spends time recreating outdoors. They still frolic in their ancient pagan beliefs, be it walking along a stone-laid labyrinth or coming together as a community in picking berries and mushrooms.

Photo by Malene Thyssen, Grib Forest, northern part of Sealand, Denmark.

Unlike much of the world, they were late in the game of moving from the comfy confines of the woods to more urban settings. According to the book, *The Nature Fix*, the Finnish score high in global scales of happiness surrounded by lakes, forests and coastlines, as well as state-sanctioned vacations.

There are no barriers even on private land, no trespassing as the Finns can roam free frolicking in nature, the only rule—no cutting of trees or hunting of game.

But it was bound to happen, the dreaded computer screens have imprisoned many Finns and as a consequence, their level of stress and obesity has increased as their amount of exercise has decreased. Their country relies on a state-run health care system, so it was important to find a cure.

New York Central Park

The city of Helsinki built a managed park much like New York's Central Park with manicured landscapes, tall pines and thick areas of rambled wilderness. Researchers discovered that visitors benefitted with just fifteen to forty-five minutes walking or jogging in the Helsinki park.

Five hours per month is the lowest amount of time to gain the preferred effect. That would be thirty minutes a couple of times a week, or for even better results, ten hours a month with five days of thirty-minute nature indulgence.

You have to admit this isn't anything new; it wasn't long ago, just a generation or two that our grandparents and great-grandparents lived on farms. They lived off the land, ate organic vegetables, butchered their own meat and sought natural herbs and remedies for ailments. Built their own barn and homes, exercise without a gym, and how ironic that today we mimic the same seeking the natural way of life. Even the literary legends of Henry David Thoreau and John Muir worshiped the same.

HELEN'S FURY

Doctors are quick to tell you to rest, presumably indoors after surgery, an auto accident or spill down the stairs, but never do they scribble the words, "go outside and get some sun."

When I was young and suffered from an illness, my mother would always tell me to change out of my pajamas and sit outside under a tree. She would bring ice tea and freshly baked bread, and it was the cure. Now we bury our heads in our phones or computer determined to self-diagnosis our sore throat into a life-threatening event.

My mother lived in a beautiful home in New Orleans, well cared for on the grounds of what was once a plantation estate. The grove of oaks sang a melody of cicadas in the warm months, a sound that always made her smile. Afflicted with Alzheimer's, and a vocabulary on the level of a preschooler at best, her love for the outdoors never waned. It was her brand of medicine.

Butterflies are messengers from past loved ones

The home has a beautiful courtyard filled with the healing chemistry of fresh air, a thriving butterfly garden and towering cypress trees filled with birdsong. My mother's eyes always told the story, she studied the landscape and her wide-eyed blues would sparkle like diamonds when she spotted those puffy clouds. Head tilted she pointed and murmured a language of lost memories, then looked deep into my eyes.

"It's going to rain momma, look at those clouds moving," I told her with anxious anticipation. She smiled and shook her head. It is the language of nature, her childhood memories of Arkansas storms. A lesson she learned from her mother in how to detect bad weather. Always look at the clouds, her mother would tell her.

When in bed she never laid facing the wall, always the window, and always looking at the sky. Just what Florence Nightingale professed in her nursing textbook more than one hundred years ago, "…like a plant, they always face the light."

In the latter months, she was on the level of an infant with loss of any viable language except crying or rapid eye movement, but she still loved staring at the trees and sky. Be it a smile or if lucky, pointing a figure to the heavens, it brought joy to my heart.

Her last day on earth was a hot day in July; the entire family was there in her room as she gasped for air. I rolled up the shades hoping she would recognize the sky while the soothing light poured into the room. I whispered into her ear, "Momma, the clouds are waiting for you, waiting to take you on an amazing ride, way up high into heaven."

I firmly believe in her last hours she was one with the clouds. A baptism bathed in eternal love, a communion of this world and the next, and then it happened. The clouds seemed to stand at attention, tall cumulus clouds growing darker with each passing moment. Her breathing became labored and the heavens broke free with torrential rain pounding the window. As the water pelted the windowpanes she began struggling for air in her last moments of life. I couldn't help wonder, was it angst or a surge of energy? Her body calmed, we each said our last goodbye, and just as she drew her last breath, the rain stopped.

Soon after, the sun struggled to come out but instead gave way to a hazy sky drenched in muted pastels. Upon leaving we learned many parts of New Orleans flooded that day, an unusual burst of angry rain that just didn't want to leave. Couldn't help but wonder if that was my momma going a little overboard with her Bon Voyage.

GREG WILKEY'S REDEMPTION

Greg Wilkey was in his forties when he lost his wife, Alicyn. Both worked in education, she a schoolteacher and Greg an assistant principal. Alicyn was at school when she collapsed with no warning, there one minute and gone the next. Greg was not with her; so no goodbyes just complete shock.

He not only lost his wife, he lost his identity and so he shared his grief on social media. Like one big family he emptied his heart, but soon realized it wasn't enough. I asked him to share his journey from tragedy to healing. A man who admits his heart rules his head and confessed that when he lost Alicyn, he was immobilized with fear and panic. His wife was the one who he turned to for guidance, his anchor when the waters got rough. And now more than ever he needed her and she was gone.

Greg is also a successful author and has written several books geared to the young adult audience. He soon turned to the written word for solace but admitted it still wasn't enough. And what do you do when your home is no longer a sanctuary, when the rooms are silent, void of any life. As Greg described, "Rooms so immense they would surely swallow me whole, rooms heavy with the weight of her absence."

When he began to dread going home, he knew it was time to do something, time to start walking, to start moving, to breathe fresh air. And so began a new Greg with a compulsive desire to walk, a driving force in his life but oddly enough a new one as he wasn't a huge nature lover.

There was a park just two miles from Greg's house and although he had passed it a thousand times, he never stopped to visit. The park was a new frontier, what Greg called his walking therapy where he discovered a connection to nature. It was his escape from all the grief and anxieties. Surrounded by life, be it wildlife or the families there, it was what he called, "something magical, comforting, being outside in the fresh air with the sunshine."

It was there Greg realized he was just one tiny speck on the planet, and although he may have been by himself, he was not alone. It was a major turning point in the healing process in living a life without his Alicyn.

He built up his walking routine, what he calls daily vacations from life, starting with a one-mile trek that gradually built up to a four to six-mile walk. Then the walks evolved into a conversation with Alicyn, sharing everything that had happened, how much he missed her and some apologies for petty arguments that they may have had. Even begging her forgiveness for all the mistakes he made during their twenty-five years together.

Through miles of tears and confessions, he found peace and acceptance in facing the trials and tribulations of his loss. It was then Greg said, "I finally understood that it was, in fact, a new world that required a new me."

Each step brought him closer to healing, away from the pain, away from what he called grief and darkness. He concentrated on the earth under his feet counting the steps moving further and further away from that moment he lost her. And then he realized each step moved him in a different direction, the day he would see her again.

Like most kids who live in the south, Greg played outdoors during those long days of summer. In his backyard was a huge oak tree, enormous he said, with branches that touched the sky. It was a tree of memories, his loving escape.

He recalled those times when he and his friends would climb the tree, and each summer they would move higher and higher. Hanging out all day sitting on the branches sharing dreams and heartfelt stories.

The tree in the photo isn't the oak Greg climbed in his youth, but definitely a place to dream about his Alicyn.

The tree is still there, still in his mother's backyard. He often wonders if the tree misses him as much as he misses its broad branches. And perhaps now the tree will take on a new meaning, closer to the heavens above, closer to his Alicyn.

"Maybe I'll just take a climb the next time I'm over there," he said reminiscing. "It'd be like spending time with an old friend."

❧ 6 ❧

BACK HOME

New Orleans City Park

In New Orleans the mighty oaks refuse to bow down to the encroaching neighborhoods and instead become partners among the century-old homes. Their loving arms bring shade to the exhaustive heat while their exposed nubby roots peel away sidewalks. Many homeowners offer a decorative flair by planting shade-loving flowers inside the crevices of the roots.

The oaks give the city character and charm; they are the romance, the voluptuous bosom of a Bourbon Street stripper, and inside the parks they are the soldiers of solitude. It is there people go for solace, for healing, to cry, to laugh, to caress and an occasional nap among the loving roots that rise above the dusty floor.

Forget the GPS, unless there's an app for oak-lined lanes. Once littered with bayous and plantations, New Orleans is blessed with shaded streets inked with marbled shadows of light, all courtesy of sprawling oaks. Esplanade Avenue is a prime example resting on the historic Esplanade Ridge dotted with stunning nineteenth-century and early twentieth-century homes.

Between Broad Avenue and City Park, there is enough to keep you busy for weeks on end. You may be calling a real estate agent and canceling your flight back home after tours of historic homes, walking through St. Louis Cemetery No. 3, kayaking Bayou St. John and jamming to the beat of the nearby Jazz & Heritage Festival.

CITY PARK

City Park is the grand dame of live oak forests with the largest grove of mature live oaks in the world with trees dating back 800 years. According to the City Park website, some of their limbs are twice as long as the height of the oak.

These mighty warriors found their seeds along a tributary of the great Mississippi River called Bayou Metairie. Indians often camped along this bayou hundreds of years ago. The park's website recants the remnants of this ancient forest, the McDonogh Oak, Anseman Oak and Suicide Oak. Mature oaks already graced the grounds in the 1800s when people began using the grounds as a park in the 100-acre tract once known as the Allard Plantation.

It is the nation's oldest urban park with its roots taking hold in 1854 where dueling gents are replaced with the New Orleans

Museum of Art, the Botanical Garden and the Carousel Amusement park including a century-old merry-go-round with hand-carved "flying horses." Today's 1300-acre park received a hefty investment during the Roosevelt Administration investing $12 million during the Works Program Administration (W.P.A.). More oaks were planted and much of the roadways, fountains, bridges and even Tad Gormley Stadium were built during this time employing 20,000 men and women.

Enrique Alferez Oak in City Park's Botanical Garden

In 1983 an inventory of the oaks found 250 trees with a circumference of over ten feet, which qualified them for entry into the Live Oak Society. The happy oaks continue to be measured each year after adding several feet in circumference along with a growing crown. Locals recognize the Enrique Alferez Oak in the park's botanical garden dressed in blue lights during the park's Celebration of the Oaks event during the holidays.

The mighty oak earns such a loving tribute based on its degree of healing and ability to live alone. Given enough room to spread its branches it is more resilient than most trees and can live for hundreds of years.

Hurricane Katrina was a devastating blow to City Park. Ninety-percent of the park, an area bigger than New York's Central Park, was underwater consumed with floodwaters caused by levee failures killing many of the younger oaks. More than 2,000 trees were killed and more than 5,000 trees replanted, but the old grove along the Bayou Metairie ridge was high and dry. Today the park is home to 30,000 trees filled with an abundance of outdoor activities for young and old. One of their newest additions since Hurricane Katrina is the wildflower pastures popular for family and bridal photos.

Just like any tragedy in life, there are lessons to be learned, and often it means going back to the root of the problem. New Orleans is known for its celebrated stubbornness to preserve its culture, its historic architecture and old infrastructure. With it means a lot of energy to maintain a city so dearly loved by people across the world. A member of The Trust for Public Land's Climate-Smart Cities program, New Orleans realized the city's catastrophe provided a blank slate of sorts to begin a more eco-friendly city.

New Orleans City park 800 year old McDonough oak

As noted on The Trust for Public Lands website, many volunteers came together adding more green space to a broken city. Besides the aesthetic appeal, it's a critical element in managing the city's storm water along with climate-related challenges with encroaching heat. As climate scientists predict an on-going increase of severe weather events, urban planners need to make changes to prepare their communities.

The Climate-Smart Cities program calls for four strategies in developing climate-resilient cities. Connect the city with more walking/biking trails to help reduce carbon emissions, add more green space such as parks, tree canopies and rooftop gardens to cool the urban landscapes, as well as replace asphalt with porous pavement in schools, playgrounds and parks. Lastly, protect coastal and river cities with flooding by conserving natural landscapes inviting communities to spend more time outdoors.

All of these elements were utilized in the New Orleans reconstruction project that continues today twelve years after the storm. The Trust for Public Lands focused on fifty acres near the entrance of City Park transforming an abandoned golf course into an open meadow with hiking and biking paths. And then the amazing success story of the park's Couturie Forest. A somewhat hidden gem, this urban park suffered significant damage after the hurricane.

But with it came renewal, a new ecosystem, and an excellent study in the healing power of forested landscapes. After the most destructive hurricane in the United States, a walk inside the wooded tundra reveals a compelling journey. In what would become an all too familiar scene in a post-K world, the forest laid barren in a dismal montage of broken trees laid to rest across an ashy-muddied landscape. The few trees that remained appeared exhausted stripped of leaves and barely anchored in the ground. It was another New Orleans treasure lost by this wicked storm.

Like so many comeback stories, it was the heart and determination of thousands of volunteers that helped bring this forest back to life. The storm helped eradicated invasive species and volunteers planted two thousand trees. Couturie Forest doubled its size from thirty acres to a sixty-acre forest in the heart of a major city; it is a peek into the city's past, a microcosm of life before urban development. Complete with an island, wildlife and scenic waterways, the trails bring to life much of what you would see on some of the nature tours south of the city.

Step inside a shaded oak forest drenched in emerald green, from the oak's majestic crowns to a sweeping mix of a wild understory. A scene reminiscent of ancient forests where fairy tales are born, perhaps King Arthur or Robin Hood and his Merry Men. Towering pines filter pools of light on a trail covered in russet-colored pine needles, especially poignant on a late afternoon stroll. Take time to study the geometric pattern of a pine's bark, they love the attention.

Don't forget to listen, listen to the sounds of the forest, those long lyrics of bird song echoed across the branches. So soothing but yet without any real translation. As the sun swings low, catch the fluttering banner of birds roosting in the trees, or the random rooster calling his flock back home.

Follow the Arboretum trail and spy the namesake of New Orleans pride, its mystical waterways, in this case, a lagoon home to cypress trees and their knobby knees peeking through the dark waters. With it dozens of brown pelicans, the state's bird, flying overhead and skimming the water. Then as the morning sun wanes, they perch themselves for a little rest and relaxation.

Stop for a little meditation at an observation deck with wooden benches nearby. Deeper inside the forest is the Laborde Lookout, a concrete sitting area that reaches forty-three feet above sea level. Looking down on the circular design, embedded in the concrete, is an etching of the city's liquid landscape, New Orleans' lifeline, the curvaceous Mississippi River.

City Park has definitely done its part in going "green," the park also constructed a wetland to divert one-third of the stormwater drain-off from a fifty-acre site that was previously a golf course.

A WORLD TURNED UPSIDE DOWN

Katrina backyard/woods damage, more than 200 trees lost

Artists and writers will tell you their most creative work rises from the ashes of despair. War, protest, natural disasters, we escape inside the canvas and blank screen seeking therapy for a bruised soul.

How ironic that we measure our lives and future against the latest disaster, and how lost we are without the urban conveniences. It is then we realize how far removed we are from our ancestors, for some just one generation removed. And so is my story in how Hurricane Katrina brought me back to my childhood, back to the spiritual power of nature, back to the wild. The only way to wash away the tears was to write, no computer, just paper and pen. This is my story...

A monster hurricane is churning the waters of the Gulf of Mexico at a clip of 175 mph. Less than twenty-four hours before landfall, August 28, 2005, Hurricane Katrina is making a beeline for our home located thirty-five miles north of New Orleans. My husband, Michael, and I decide to stay close and evacuate thirty miles north to the town of Folsom.

We own six acres shrouded in ten-story pines and a creek teeming with fish, turtles and egrets. Our journey began in 1979 as weekend warriors for six long years carving a road, bridge and home. Blood, sweat and tears literally went into our homestead. It was more than a home, it was like a family member, and we didn't want to leave.

As we pulled away I took one last look. My husband built her strong but she had trees just inches away. We put the recliner, television, and keepsakes in the middle of the living room and covered it with heavy-duty tarps. Somehow we felt convinced that if the roof caved in our valuables would be intact.

Backyard/woods before Katrina

We stockpiled enough provisions for three days and loaded up the cat and dog. People from southeastern Louisiana to southern Mississippi fled with little more than the clothes on their backs. Many thought they would return in a couple of days. Some never did, moving their families further north, while others never lived to tell their story.

Hunkered down in Folsom, the winds started to howl at daybreak and we retreated to an interior room listening to the constant bombing of branches and trees. Outside it looked like a combat zone, a barrage of snapped light poles and uprooted trees wreaking havoc along the roadways.

Morning after Katrina hit

Loaded with chainsaws and heavy ropes, men moved sections of debris with pickup trucks and tractors. Ladies criss-crossed the littered roads in four-wheelers delivering water and food. For miles it was a rerun of devastation, trees on homes, cars and barns.

Backroads 65 miles north of New Orleans

I couldn't help thinking, "We have so many trees, how could they miss, how could we possibly have a home?"

There was no power, no forms of communication, we were all pioneers left to fend for ourselves.

On August 31, two days after the storm, we found our way back home.

Zigzagging a maze of mangled trees, we travel the back roads lined with shattered forests. Closer to town the interstates show signs of exhaustion with mutilated signs and severed billboards. My stomach started to sink.

We turn into our narrow dead-end road and forced to park. Our lush forest is pulverized with broken pines, uprooted hardwoods and trees stripped of leaves. Michael puts his arm around me and we trek down the road. He hacks a path inside a mound of broken branches and we make our way to the creek. On the other side is our home and property, but the jumbled debris blocks our view.

"You stay here, I'm going in to see if it's still there," he said giving me a firm warning as he wormed his way through our battered forest.

At my feet, the flooded creek spawns pools of dying perch flopping furiously trying to find a water source. I place a rag over my face to block the stench of stagnant water and rotting fish basking in the broiling sun.

My mind wanders in the fate of other wildlife, "Where did they go, the deer, foxes, raccoons? Will they come back?"

I can't stand the waiting and ignore the orders and battle my way through the crown of a fallen tree.

Wearing a t-shirt, long jeans and old tennis shoes, I crush the branches with my hands and feet trying to keep my balance. Water squishes through my toes and my arms bleed sliced by the sharp edges of severed branches, but the adrenaline keeps me going until I finally break through.

Paralyzed at the sight, I couldn't breath; I couldn't even cry, it was utter destruction. Hundreds of trees dead, and the thought of mourning such a tragedy seemed selfish when so many lost much more.

The beginning of a long journey in restoring our home and losing more than 200 trees. And we were one of the lucky ones.

Through the shattered mess I see a blur of the house, and then Michael walking towards me.

Tears streaming down his face he is overjoyed, "It's still here! It's still here!"

He mumbles something about his carpentry skills, how he built the house and how proud he was that it was still standing.

Just one week before Katrina we moved our son to college with his sister and became empty nesters. And now we are parents again. Our tiny piece of heaven was a tattered scene from hell and our property, our creation, was crying for help.

Five tons of trees crashed through the attic and second story but the house stood strong and didn't collapse. But how long could it hang on with all that weight? Luckily, two weeks after the storm we found a skilled team who peeled the trees off our roof one section at a time.

Insurance would pay for the home but not the yard. We immediately rid the home of soaked carpet and damaged materials to prevent mold and further damage. Although we hired a contractor, it wasn't until the new year before they could start.

The next task at hand was an unforgiving, yet gratifying lesson in survival camping out for a month on the first floor of our home. With an all-electric home and an underground well, we had no air, water, phone, television or internet, and no means of cooking or washing. Michael was in rare form, master of his domain with his construction skills and pure strength.

We borrowed a generator and ran the lines through the bottom of the fireplace into the house. There we had a safe and organized set of cords and power strips. The refrigerator was emptied and replaced with bare necessities. With gas more than $4 a gallon; Michael organized a strict generator schedule for fans, refrigerator, charging flashlights, and an occasional peek at the television. Our meals were limited to sandwiches, salads and grilled meats on the gas barbecue pit.

And without water, we rationed flushing using rainwater and the neighbor's pool water. Baths were a bit more creative, I learned to bath with one gallon of water warmed by the scorching sun on the back deck. Clothes were cleaned in the bathtub with a bare minimum of water and hung to dry on a homemade clothesline.

We discovered the lost art of conversation and worked from dawn to dusk like the early days constantly cutting and clearing bringing normalcy in a world turned upside down.

After days of humming chainsaws and aching muscles moving branches the size of small trees, we spy a familiar sight, a small patch of green, the rebirth of a dying spirit.

With sweat pouring down his face he looked at the green grass and said, "Now that's a beautiful thing." And I shook my head, swallowing the lump in my throat wiping away the tears.

Three weeks later Michael went back to work and for months I continued moving debris. My faithful pooch, Spikey, kept me company and sometimes when I would break down crying, he would nudge me barking orders to get back to work. In January three different church groups from across the country gave up their vacation and college break to help clear broken trees, branches and tons of pine needles.

Spring 2006, the beginning of nature's healing. She came back with a vengeance

By late spring 2006, the house was finished with a new roof, floors, ceilings and newly painted walls. We rescued our home and property, brought it back to life, and stayed true to a promise we made a long time ago.

Our homestead began with just one acre cleared leaving the majority of acreage in the hands of nature. It took twenty years to develop maintenance-free, shade-tolerant gardens, free of fertilizers and weed killers, just an occasional pruning. I added mostly native species including sixty azalea bushes and brought in family heirloom Louisiana Irises. And in one day it was all gone.

Today, thanks to the added light, I have a butterfly, vegetable and herb garden. Butterflies and hummingbirds feast on the althea and zinnias while tomatoes and peppers worship the sun. Every day I inspect the mint, lavender, thyme, oregano, parsley and admire the cilantro growing tall with blossoms. I plant enough for the occasional caterpillar to eat his way into a cocoon while the lizards busy themselves eating insects.

The wildlife has returned with a vengeance. Besides our growing deer population, there are rabbits, foxes, raccoons, possums and armadillos, and a rise in coyotes. Due to the many dead trees still standing, there are numerous woodpecker colonies. The increased clearing has also invited more hawks, bluebirds and many migrating birds.

My mother's heirloom iris refused to bloom until after Katrina

It's been more than 30 years since my husband and I took that first walk across the creek. We nurtured the property through floods, tornadoes and hurricanes. The home is like new and my gardens and wildlife are blossoming. There are still signs of Katrina especially in the winter but thanks to Mother Nature we now have thirty-foot willow trees, new live oaks and river oaks, as well as dozens of pine seedlings. It's a different paradise, a little rough around the edges, but built with more than thirty years of love and devotion.

SOLDIER OF THE BAYOUS

A Cajun author, photographer, and lecturer Greg Guirard's family set homestead at the turn of the twentieth century outside the small town of Catahoula. He lived on the fringe of the Atchafalaya Basin with a bayou skirting the property and the basin's levee in plain view. He worked the land until the day he died, building furniture out of sinker cypress, and going inside the bayous for crawfish, photographs, and peace of mind.

Fellow mentor and friend, Greg gifted me with his book Atchafalaya Autumn II published in October 2010. The book echoes much of my visits to his homestead and my sister's nearby home. My sister, Michelle Guirard is married to Greg's nephew, Ed Guirard. Reminiscent of Thoreau's journals, only a bit more southern, Greg paints vibrant images of boney cypress clutching spiraling moss, a beaver nursing its young, gators sunning their hides with bald eagles and swallowtail kites soaring the skies.

Beaver nest with mom and her baby in the Atchafalaya Basin

Set in the autumn months, his photographs highlight sunrises and sunsets with scorching ribbons of clouds in a fiery canvas of orange, pinks and reds. The book spans two decades of Greg's travels introducing readers to the basin and its people. Peppered with quotes from Henry David Thoreau and William Faulkner, he uses a line from Thoreau in describing his journey, "I went to the woods because I wished to live deliberately…"

He built a platform for his camera and tripod at Lake Fausse Pointe among a group of three cypress trees overlooking a corridor of trees. Unlike artists, photographers are at the whim of nature's moods. Catching that perfect sunrise is not a chance meeting. It can be a painstaking process racing to the platform several times fighting the dark, cold and sometimes foggy waters.

And finally, a prized photo, what Greg called a gift, albeit a brief one. The sun slides through a narrow slit on the horizon framed by weeping moss. It's a quick peek as a blue heron perches on a stump inside the shaft of orange sunlight. Another photo brings to life the late afternoon glow splashing across a flock of white pelicans and a curvaceous cypress tree bathed in the light of a full moon. In addition to the visual splendor, Greg shares the swamp's sweet songs: the early morning call of geese, ducks whistling over the trees, cormorant and anhinga feeding on the water.

The Atchafalaya Basin holds over 170 species of birds, some with wingspans of eight feet or more. Skilled fishermen catch catfish over five feet and garfish more than ten feet, alligators eleven to fifteen foot long weighing a ton and turtles at 100 pounds. Beavers, nutria, mink, otters, deer, bobcats, coyotes, Louisiana panther and the threatened Louisiana Black Bear all make the Basin their home.

Moved by the Basin's infinite beauty and dedicated to Faulkner's stewardship of preservation, Greg shared the sights and sounds in seven self-published books. He, like all of us, worship the magic of the Atchafalaya Basin. "There is an almost mystical connection between Cajun fisherman and the swamp, a desire not only to see but to touch, to be part of the wilderness...to be in concert with the big woods."

Greg Guirard's houseboat, he would bring the boat deep inside the bayous to take photos and pen his prose

His words and rich photographs paint a comforting but surreal experience as he muses about the decimation of the great cypress forest and today's urban sprawl. Greg bemoans the mortality of the Basin in his book, "We assume nature can take care of itself. That it can renew somehow. We fail to realize its needs are our needs."

Greg Guirard died suddenly at the age of 80 on June 2, 2017. Still in his prime caring for his forests and reseeding his kingdom with young trees, he left his mark and his legend. He will never be forgotten.

Thoreau believed trees were a symbol of immortality, and so is Greg Guirard in the eyes of those who loved him. In a tribute to this extraordinary man, I wrote a eulogy dedicated to his forever spirit.

He's Still Here

He is deep in our hearts, that Cajun voice with a heavy drawl

He is here in Bayou Amy, the old twines and broken pumps

He is here in the soul of every tree, giving so many new life

He is here in every grain of wood, his forever lifeline

He is here in every boat ride, the magic finds of beaver nests

He is here in every blade of grass, the grass he never cut

He is here in every book, his words forever echoed in our minds

He is here in every photograph, his passion and wild adventures

He is here in every crawfish, walking slowing in time with the tide

He is here to stay, forever in our hearts, wherever we may go

THE SEASONS OF THE SWAMP

In Thoreau's passage titled Walking printed in the book, *Thoreau and the Language of Trees*, author Richard Higgins does an excellent job in painting a picture of Thoreau's life living in what he called a sacred place. What a joyous moment when I read this passage, as four years ago I titled my series of books under the same name, Sacred Places.

Thoreau wrote, "When I would recreate myself, I seek the darkest wood, the thickest and most interminable, and, to the citizen, most dismal swamp. I enter a swamp as a sacred place—a sanctum sanctorum."

I too agree the swamp is sacred, and a reminder of our primeval confines. Where the alligator is king and still holds its ancient profile, its rugged hide with nary an enemy except for man. In this next essay, I share both a personal and spiritual journey of discovery in search of a forest rarely seen; it is there I found my creative gift.

Photography is a personal, intimate form of art, the photographer and camera become one in a desperate attempt to capture a moment, a single glimpse of life and an eternal memory. This art form is mobile assembling many to new worlds and forging unique relationships.

Photographs warm hearts, resurrect forgotten souls and enlighten the spirits of those who witness its timeless beauty.

It is this style of art and passion that brought a new chapter to my life igniting an everlasting bond between my father and I. My father discovered a new love, a captivating and elusive treasure that gains its beauty from isolated terrain and winding waterways. It was the Maurepas Swamp that cast a forbidding spell, taunting us to glide beneath her canopy of tangled trees welcoming the watchful eye of my camera.

So we began a journey down these rivers with my father's eyes guiding me and the camera's eye savoring the virtuous waters. It's a fiery commitment to steal a slice of this endless wonderland, tucking it deep into our hearts seeking refuge from time itself.

Nature controls our every mood, from the wide-open skies to the insects that crawl the forest floor or the harsh fury of a thunderstorm to the delicate wings of a butterfly. They can be altered by the vision of a lone tree in an open field or a rolling hill filled with flowers blowing in the wind.

The click of the shutter can excite the senses or yield a pristine peace. Together the camera and my infinite curiosity deliver a spiritual awakening into the secrets of the river and its forgotten legends.

I came to know this land in the 70s and 80s when my father built a camp on the Amite River. In my twenties single and full of vigor, all my energies were dedicated to documenting the wonders of this land. Now more than three decades later, I return to Livingston Parish and once more get lost inside the elusive waters of the Amite River, Blind River, Black River and Chinquapin Canal.

The water is a mirror reflecting every ray of light, forming a kaleidoscope of color, while the cypress knees form a burial ground all resurrected by the single click of a shutter. Dead trees intermix with seedlings fighting for light to survive and ominous shadows dance between the rotten limbs. These waterways penetrate my soul leaving a heavenly addiction captivating this enchanted land.

Swamps and bayous offer a poetic stage in sharing the seasons of our lives, nature's drama entwined with Maurepas' own personalities.

It's a peaceful journey for those who long for the innocence of a bygone era.

Strangers in a mystical land, I am sensitive to the swamp's unique and fragile beauty. Some of her friends are shy and forbidding while others seem to welcome the camera's dutiful eye. Maurepas holds a formidable force and her power can be unleashed at any moment.

There's a peace the rivers bring, a visual drama that humbles all who enter. Invigorated by the iridescent colors of a sunset after a cloudy afternoon, it's a canvas that artists replicate time and time again. But perhaps nothing is more illuminating than Black River and its inexhaustible reflections.

Water black as Louisiana crude washes against the emerald palmettos that fan the shores. A purple blur whisks across the horizon passing a prairie of water hyacinths glowing in the sun. The irises and spider lilies playfully hug each other along the river's banks. There is a harmony of wildlife amid Maurepas' varied personalities, from turbulent weather to abundant food chains, the camera lens struggles with the changing weather and light. Perhaps the swamp enjoys this playful game of chase.

After several years of stalking the water, my ever-changing companion begins to reveal her secrets. Pay close attention as the swamp signals changes in the weather; white anvil clouds yield thunderheads, brisk winds precede a calm before a storm, and the animals grow quiet before a hurricane. We became partners in this natural drama; the rivers surrender their beauty while my pictures tell their story.

The back rivers and bayous are the only place in Louisiana that brings waves of color with every season. Spring delivers a renewal of life with a backdrop of bright green leaves while the water explodes into a rainbow of color. Irises, lilies, lotuses, morning glories, cypress vines and the swamp rose, all awaken the desolate brown and grey tones of winter. A cadence of shutter clicks echoes through the trees as the macro lens discovers an erotic love affair between a bumblebee and a flower's sweet juices.

Front blowing through a cypress forest

Summer evokes energy with the fusion of sweltering heat, angry storms, and bursts of pelting rain. Nature's nourishing waters feed the swamp's shoreline painted in a gratuitous green, a reminder of her sovereign spirit. Suddenly a union of sky and horizon, the water mirroring the puffy clouds above as if the world turned upside down. Lazy turtles line the rivers, sunning themselves in the oppressive heat, an easy target for my camera's eye as well as the gator's prowl.

Senses so heightened even the darkness of the closing shutter invites a hypnotic trance that mindless space of time, a crescendo of emotions that you pray will never end. But soon a wave of loneliness, summer is coming to an end. August brings a weary presence; trees heavy with blemished leaves are growing tired of the relentless heat and whisper the winds of autumn.

Cypress trees turn a deep russet while maples and gums are adorned with a bright red crown of leaves. Like a sweeping fire of autumn colored flames, sunsets join the party giving birth to layers of iridescent orange and yellow. Soon daybreak brings a haunting effect as a grey mist falls heavy on the forests. There's that familiar pain watching the aging cypress knowing it will soon be over, but memories of the crisp cool air and the smell of burning leaves bring the camp back into focus.

A desolate calm falls on my rivers during the winter. The barren cypress trees extend their long bony fingers toward the heavens. Cypress knees pirouette through the waters emphasizing their grace and beauty in the stillness of the swamp. Abandoned fishing sheds torn from the summer storms appear naked and weary from their season's rewards.

Winter fronts cast ominous streams of clouds forming a ceiling of color. Fiery reds burn the lens with a look of penetrating heat swallowing all dimensions except for the lone fisherman. Red cardinals bring a delightful contrast against the washed blur of gray; perhaps they bring a message of admiration for my father who kept their feeders stocked during the brash winter.

This passage is a testament to my father and Maurepas; thankful for the lessons he and the waters have taught me. A testament to a renewed spirit of an old friend, my father guiding me one more time to see the beauty, to tell the tale. I hear his call and stay committed with a promise that everyone will come to know the beauty and enchantment we found, my voice will be heard for many generations to come.

Ansel Adams reminds us, "Photography has an obligation to help us see more clearly and more deeply and to reveal to others the grandeur and potentials of the one and only world we inhabit."

✤ 7 ✤

RECLAIMING LOST FORESTS

Sinker Cypress in Atchafalaya Basin

I n the mid-70s, supporting a wife and four children on a teacher's salary, Greg Guirard began to fall deeper in debt and turned to his native land for help. He quit teaching and began collecting driftwood and sinker cypress logs earning a living making furniture.

When the virgin cypress forests were cut in the nineteenth and early twentieth century, many were lost in the water. They are called sinkers because they were not supported by barrels or floatation devices and sank. Cypress contains a good deal of oil resulting in a very dense wood resistant to rot and termites.

The ancient cypress forests were logged at the turn of the 20th century, today the younger versions line the Louisiana bayous

Guirard has pulled hundreds of sinker logs ranging from eighteen to thirty-six inches in diameter. The longest piece was eighty-two feet long, and one sixty-foot piece was straight as a ruler. Harvesting sinker cypress connected him to a time when the Basin towered with virgin cypress rising 120 to 140-foot tall and a girth of eight to nine feet in diameter.

Most locals work the narrow bayous with a standard aluminum boat normally sixteen to seventeen-foot long with a forty-horsepower motor. It's small enough to weave inside the swamp but strong enough to haul the cypress logs back to the dock. Guirard hunted sinker cypress when the water table was very low.

"I mostly find them walking across the bottom of the swamp. I tie them up, then attach a pontoon or large piece of styrofoam to one end of the log," he explained noting they are too heavy to move. "I leave the log tied there until spring when the waters float it high enough so I can pull it out with my boat."

It can take four to six hours hauling the heavy logs back to the launch depending on location, size and number. Using his pickup truck he guided the trailer down the boat ramp until it was almost completely covered in water. He then moved the floating logs onto the trailer and headed back to the swamp for more logs. "I usually load it up with three or four logs and bring them straight to the mill sopping wet," he said.

His offsite storage facility is home to many pieces of wood. Stacked horizontally each is unique in color, pattern and weight as each tree owns its own personality. A closer look reveals slanted ax marks on some of the pieces that could mean a tree cut prior to the Civil War. Guirard explains, "If the big end of a log is cut slanted rather than straight-across, it usually means the tree was cut down before the U.S. Civil War since crosscut saws were used almost exclusively after the War."

Thanks to Greg's hard work and Cajun craftsmanship, much of this old-growth cypress will live forever in furniture passed down by generations of families.

ANCIENT FOREST RESURRECTED

Photo by John J. O'Brien courtesy of Wikimedia Commons.

In examining the mystical world of trees we have explored the symbiotic relationship between trees and man. We have learned the forest is also a barometer of the health of our environment. And of course, we mourn the destruction of all forests, especially our ancient forests. Imagine the delight of scientists and environmentalists in discovering the resurrection of a prehistoric forest in the Gulf of Mexico.

Dive shop owner Chas Broughton received phone calls from locals reporting active marine life in an area that is normally filled with starfish and jellyfish. So Broughton went out to take a look. It was there, sixty feet underwater just south of Gulf Shores, Alabama, he found what he said looked like a prehistoric riverbed surrounded by trees. A sight he admitted was quite different from his usual dives in the Gulf of Mexico over the last twenty-five years. Broughton then hired environmental journalist Ben Raines to help him research this cypress forest on the bottom of the Gulf.

A thirty-minute documentary brings the viewer alongside the diver to witness this American Atlantis. Much like a crystal ball, the diver embarks on a journey that will soon forever change what we know about our environmental landscape. In anxious anticipation, the crystal clear waters reveal an ancient forest. The roots and jagged pieces of tree trunks crawl along the ocean floor, thousands of trees rooted in the dirt where they grew 60,000 years ago.

The documentary, The Underwater Forest, written and directed by environmental writer Ben Raines, calls it "a wholly unique relic of our planet's past, the only known site where a coastal ice age forest this old has been preserved in place."

This swampy forest was buried in mud, layers of what scientists believe were the result of rising sea levels. And so the trees were protected by decomposition buried in a hermetically sealed grave. Some of the trees owned a circumference of close to thirty feet, which rivaled the California redwoods.

Marshy waters near the Gulf of Mexico

Ironically Hurricane Ivan, another natural phenomenon, uncovered the relics. Nicknamed Ivan the Terrible, the storm raged through the Gulf as a Category 5 hurricane in 2004 and tore through the Alabama and Florida Gulf Coast. Waves reaching ninety-eight-feet tall were recorded with offshore data buoys, but that was before the buoys were ripped from their moorings by fierce winds. The eye passed directly over the location of the forest. It was Ivan that broke the seal of this underwater time capsule and gave new life to this prehistoric forest.

Below the Gulf's green water is a tropical wonderland, quite the opposite of its usual flat sandy bottom. When the forested landscape was set free by the storm, it became a coral reef. The video reveals a scene much like a National Geographic special, strange looking crabs with long spindly legs bounce across the cypress roots while sponges sprout from old stumps, sea turtles glide along the ruins and a vast carpet of sea anemones cling to the tree bark. Raines commented that every crevice of the tree stumps and roots were a conclave for small fish. Even a fluorescent nocturnal fish, the flame cardinalfish, was guarding its cypress-paneled home.

The two newfound explorers immediately called in scientists and researchers from local and regional universities. All were giddy in what is best described as an enormous petri dish of organisms just waiting to tell their story. A buried treasure in every grain of wood brought to the surface. Like storytellers, the trees began sharing secrets of the past, the climate, annual rainfall, insect populations and plant life that inhabited the Gulf Coast before humans roamed the earth. More importantly, how did they live and how did they die?

Just to be clear, this forest is older than the Egyptian pyramids, and some scientists estimate the forest experienced multiple ice ages. A time when sea levels were hundreds of feet lower, the earth was much cooler and most of the U.S. and the planet were covered in glaciers.

Kristine DeLong, a Louisiana State University paleoclimatologist, confirmed the dating. She sent the samples to a national laboratory for radiocarbon dating. They knew something was up when the wood was so old even the testing couldn't date them. After taking several other samples, DeLong concluded the samples were what is known as "radiocarbon dead."

A team of LSU geologists then went to the site to collect core samples from the seafloor. The sediment offered a chronology timeline based on the layers that have built up over the millennia. Using sonar machines, the LSU team found an area with a substantial amount of trees still buried in the sediment, some more than ten feet down.

Like a puzzle they put all the pieces together, the samples provided a historic trail back to a 50,000 to 60,000-year time span. A time when the Gulf shoreline was a good thirty to sixty miles further offshore than today's beaches, a time when today's islands looked like mountains. And of course, it was miles away from the Gulf because salt water kills cypress trees.

Aging cypress still lives with center gutted from his trunk

With continued research, Andy Resse, a pollinologist at the University of Southern Mississippi, revealed that the pollen extracted from the wood resembled a rare forest indigenous to North and South Carolina where winters are much colder than the Gulf Coast.

Dr. Grant Harley, a dendrochronologist, from the University of Southern Mississippi, analyzed multiple wood samples studying the patterns of the rings. He was astonished in how the rings matched proving the trees grew together, and once dried, they all had a very vibrant smell with sap leaking out of the wood. Looking under a microscope, he confirmed they were tens of thousands of years old.

Like a forensic pathologist, Harley then began to research how the trees died, be it a disease, drought or insects. He learned the oldest of the ten samples was 500 years, and surrounding trees were alive at some point during that lifespan. After studying various scientific data, Harley concluded the trees most likely died of saltwater intrusion due to rising sea levels.

And many of the scientists agree. They believe that this underwater forest is concrete proof of climate change and fluctuating sea levels. Dr. Martin Becker, a paleontologist from William Patterson University can normally be found searching for shark's teeth, but not in the ocean. He was sifting 35-million-year-old shark teeth below a waterfall on an Alabama river, which was a good 100 miles from the nearest shoreline. Proof he concludes that half of the state of Alabama was at one time submerged under an ocean during the times of dinosaurs. He believes the water will return along with the sharks, but how long it will take is still a mystery.

One thing for sure, this amazing treasure will continue to educate scientists across the globe and offer clues in protecting our fragile environment. Raines admitted that his articles have gone viral and he is receiving calls from around the world. They have received so many inquiries that the Underwater Forest LLC has applied to the government to make it a National Marine Sanctuary so it will forever remain a protected site.

8

CREATIVES SHINE

A southern jewel and her pups. Photo by Christy Fitzmorris

The divine beauty of the natural world consumed environmental lords such as Ansel Adams, John Muir and Henry David Thoreau. They labored to share and protect the landscapes educating the masses with their creative talents. Each left their mark, their contribution that we continue to enjoy today.

HENRY DAVID THOREAU

Born in 1817, Thoreau found peace of mind in nature's confines. Living most of his life in and around Concord, Massachusetts, he was not terrifically social and as a child delighted in picking huckleberries with his mother. She also had a love for nature and soon Thoreau came to know the name of every crawling insect, roaming animal, along with fruit and flower. He built his own boat as a teenager and often would travel the local rivers.

As a young adult, Thoreau became good friends with Ralph Waldo Emerson, the lauded poet and writer. It was Emerson who introduced Thoreau to local writers Nathaniel Hawthorne and Louisa May Alcott. Soon Emerson suggested Thoreau keep a journal, and so he did with his first entry on October 22, 1837. It remained his constant companion penning more than two million words and fourteen volumes according to the History of Massachusetts website.

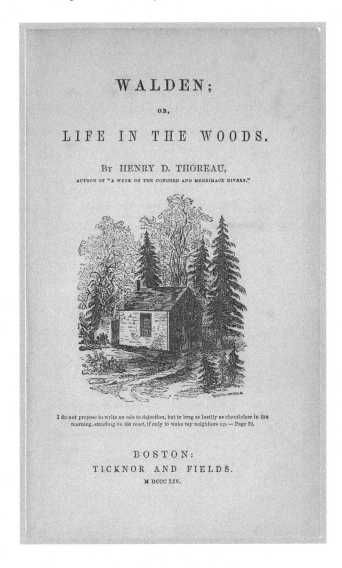

Thoreau's first book, *A Week on the Concord and Merrimack Rivers*, published in 1849 shares a two-week trip he and his brother John took during the summer of 1839. But it was the two years living on Walden Pond in March of 1845 that brought Thoreau complete bliss. It was there he wrote his first book in tribute to his brother and began his journal that would become his most famous book titled, *Walden: Or, Life in the Woods.*

The book was released in 1858 and received rave reviews. Although it was successful it took five years to sell 2,000 copies and was out of print when Thoreau died in 1862. At the age of forty-five Thoreau succumbed to tuberculosis that plagued him during college years according to the Thoreau Society website. The site notes he left a generous number of unfinished projects with records of natural phenomena around Concord with what they called extensive notes on American Indians and volumes of daily journal jottings.

As per the Thoreau Society website is a quote from Thoreau's friend, Ralph Waldo Emerson, who delivered the eulogy:

"The country knows not yet, or in the least part, how great a son it has lost. His soul was made for the noblest society; he had a short life exhausted the capabilities of this world; wherever there is knowledge, wherever there is virtue, wherever there is beauty, he will find a home."

Walden National Park, photo courtesy of Jesse Lee Tucker

In tribute to Henry David Thoreau, the state of Massachusetts has designated Walden Pond a National Historic Landmark. The state's website goes on to say that Thoreau's book *Walden* has inspired awareness and respect for the natural environment. And Walden Pond considered the birthplace of the conservation movement. The park itself is 335 acres with close to 2,680 acres of undeveloped forests that surround the reservation called Walden Woods.

ANSEL ADAMS

Ansel Adams brought to life every curve of wind-strewn hay, every wrinkle of a crusted tree trunk and every drop of collective mist across the wooded meadows. He was a romantic, a throwback from the realm of nineteenth-century American landscape painting and photography.

The Ansel Adams Gallery website also proclaimed he to be a direct philosophical heir of Ralph Waldo Emerson, Henry David Thoreau and John Muir. He lived a robust life and was an unrelenting activist in protecting the environment until his death in 1984 at the age of 82.

Adams combined his engaging personality with his talents as a compulsive communicator to build his audience. He then promoted his photography as fine art and helped in establishing the department of photography at the Museum of Modern Art in New York. From there came a growing number of contacts resulting in exhibitions, published books and his work with the Sierra Club. Adams became the icon in the promotion of national parks.

Ansel Adams Grand Teton Snake River courtesy of U.S. National Park Service

The Ansel Adams Gallery website goes on to proclaim his work and his range of involvement was "encyclopedic." Including everything from wild Alaska and his beloved Big Sur coast of California to the mighty redwoods.

Perhaps the most American artist this country has ever seen, he introduced the Wild West to millions of people that even today brings awe and conviction. Theodore Roosevelt and the president's endearing zest of Americanism also heavily influenced Adams. Today his work continues to energize the populace and to protect what Adams so masterfully documented in his photography. What the website noted was the artist's belief that man can live in harmony and balance with its environment.

"You don't make a photograph just with a camera. You bring to the act of photography all the pictures you have seen, the books you have read, the music you have heard, the people you have loved," Ansel Adams, legendary photographer and environmental activist.

JOHN MUIR

A Scottish-American, John Muir was truly devoted to the spiritual world of nature. The Public Broadcasting Station offers a thorough biography of Muir in his work in raising awareness to the critical role of our nation's environment and the need for national parks. Muir believed mankind was just a part of the integral dynamics of the natural world, but not its master.

Born in 1838, Muir moved from Dunbar, Scotland with his family to a Wisconsin farm in 1849. As a young man, he walked from Indiana to Florida drawing botanical sketches along the way. Then sailed to California and began another walking adventure from San Francisco to the Sierra Nevada. It was then his life was forever changed; he surrendered every aspiration in life to preserving nature. Muir's never-ending crusade to ignite the hearts of Americans was fueled by multi-layered landscapes and their timeless layers of light.

He preached his gospel and gained national fame writing articles for major magazines, Overland Monthly, Scribner's and Harper's Magazine. The PBS website noted that although he settled down briefly upon his marriage to Louie Wanda Strentzel, living on her family farm in Martinez California, it was the wilds of Alaska's Glacier Bay and Washington's Mount Rainier that brought a life-long addiction. Muir's writings were a prominent part in these glorious lands gaining their national park title.

Muir then championed the protection of the Petrified Forest and Grand Canyon in Arizona. These were more than nomadic adventures; Muir was a pilgrim for preservation on a mission to protect a silent but vital partner of the natural world. His poetic prose not only brought life to those who never witnessed the rugged terrain but an eternal affection that ignited the masses to join his crusade.

Photo by Normherr, Muir Lake, Sequoia National Park

Acting as a public voice for the high country around Yosemite Valley, it too was crowned with the title of a national park in 1890, along with General Grant and Sequoia National Park. Soon his work led to others fighting for the same cause and park supporters fought to make a large park in the Kings Canyon region of Central California.

Muir co-founded the Sierra Club in 1892, an environmental-advocacy organization, and served as president for more than two decades. Today, it remains a beacon for environmentalists and preservationists.

Perhaps Muir's most lauded venture was his three-night camping trip in 1903 with President Theodore Roosevelt. Muir had a captive audience from sunrise to sunset with fireside discussions under a dome of stars. Yes, Muir had a way with words, but it was nature's spirit that found Roosevelt's heart as they camped inside Yosemite National Park.

Roosevelt penned a tribute to Muir as noted on the Sierra Club website, sharing great detail on their trip in what the president described as, "...we lay in the open, the enormous cinnamon-colored trunks rising about us like the columns of a vaster and more beautiful cathedral than was ever conceived by any human architect."

Muir Woods National Monument, photo by EPoelzl, Wikimedia Commons

The most powerful man in the country was smitten by the beauty of nature and granted federal protection of the Yosemite Valley and Mariposa Big Tree, making both parts of the Yosemite National Park.

Roosevelt's words still ring true more than a century later. As scribed in the Sierra Club historical journal:

"There can be nothing in the world more beautiful than the Yosemite, the groves of the giant sequoias...our people should see to it that they are preserved for their children and their Children's children forever, with their majestic beauty all unmarred."

In 1905 California Congressman William Kent purchased 611 acres to protect a swath of the state's old-growth redwood forests. Kent then donated it to the Federal Government and President Theodore Roosevelt declared it a national monument. Kent suggested it be named for the conservationist John Muir. Today Muir Woods is one of the San Francisco Bay Areas most popular tourist attractions with 6,000 visitors per day during peak times.

CREATIVE CURE

In reading the words of Thoreau and studying Ansel Adams' legendary photography, we are all drawn to that special piece of heaven. What Wohlleben professed as the everyday miracles that a forest can bring. The greatest gift is to become one with nature, to feel her moods and to witness her everyday life. From the time one open's their eyes to bidding farewell to the silver shadows of the moon.

Earlier in the book we learned the medicinal benefits from nature, evidence continues to show that forest therapy boosts your immune system, improves mood, accelerates recovery from surgery or illness and even offers a deeper sleep at night. But more than physical, there's the mental aspect, immersing ourselves in our natural environment brings us a deeper and clearer intuition along with a renewed spirit of happiness and social interaction.

But what about our creative spirit, be it a housewife or business executive we all thrive and excel on those artistic vibes. How many times have you often wished your brain could just stop? Well not literally, but today's culture has, in essence, overloaded our sensory receptors.

Our poor little brains have had enough from commercials to

computer apps, bucket lists long enough to fill a bathtub, and don't forget those wretched beeping phones. Those billions of nerves and neurons are busy enough moving our body, and then we abuse the frontal lobe with reason, logic, spontaneity and decision-making skills. Bottom line, our brains need rest and relaxation. The insistent chatter in our heads is fueled by long hours of work, overbooked schedules, noise pollution in overcrowded cities, and even the vacations are nonstop with little rest.

All we need to do is reboot our brain, reconnect with nature and let the magic begin.

Photo by Ngresonance, part of the Wikimedia Commons project

Kris Abrams from the Cedar Tree Healing Arts Center in Boulder Colorado and her video How Nature Heals reminds us that the forest is deep within us. We've lost touch with our inner self, poisoned by our toxic culture. Our creative mind is numb as society dictates what we feel, what we believe, even standards in what is good and bad, pretty and ugly. Like robots, we lose touch with our own feelings.

Abrams reminds us that when walking nature's path, there are no imperfections, we see only beauty, no skinny or fat trees, just beautiful trees. No matter their color, their origin, even their blemished leaves, all have their own unique signature. It's an organic way of life, a slower pace; a place to surrender your soul and immerse yourself into the unknown. Around every corner, every turn brings new discoveries, and a new you.

For some, it is hard to empty the rat race brain waves. Difficult to give in to the silence, to welcome the mystery, to awaken that forgotten child, to stir those creative juices and let the mind run free. It is then Abrams reminds us the world shrinks, the problems fade and you become one with nature.

We all need the same thing, we are all one, both humans and nature. We all share similar chemical compounds, we are all one cycle of life and we cannot live without the other. When we breathe, the trees breathe, and they love our company.

Nature is buried inside us and it is nature that feeds our creative spirit. But like food, we need daily doses. To walk a wooded trail, feel the leaf litter below our feet, listen to the twigs snap and the vaulting of wildlife. Embark on a spiritual journey back to our roots, back to the innocence, and back to our real self.

For some, it is easier said than done, more than just walking in the woods with your earbuds listening to music or the latest podcast you missed. Some walk but don't listen to nature's call, instead the mind is busy with a to-do list or rehashing that conversation you had with a friend or coworker. What Abrams calls a shift from an accidental spiritual relationship to an intentional investment of time outdoors consciously connecting to Mother Nature.

We have all had them, those magical moments when we feel connected, perhaps listening to the wind whistling through the leaves or spying the morning sun spotlighting a broken tree that still lives. That's when the brain and the body change directions, when your creative spirit is one with the trees. One with the doe and fawns that stop to graze the forest.

Prince William County Forest park

Abrams also reminds us it needs to be a solitary experience, perhaps just a couple of steps away from the trail of people to fully gain the spiritual awakening. And it doesn't have to be a grand landscape, perhaps next to a creek or a visit to that broken tree that still holds life. To get the full effect, bring something to sit on, be it a yogi mat or chair, relax and let your mind rest.

Bring together all your senses studying each minute piece of your territory then let your imagination run wild. Focus on one thing that brings you peace, a tree, rock, or flower, and rather than just admiring it start a conversation out loud. Perhaps it is a question or confiding a difficult decision, but continue sharing your thoughts studying the beauty, the color, the uniqueness of the object, just as you would in talking to a person. And soon you will "hear" the answer.

Writers often talk about getting lost in the zone, that place where the words appear out of nowhere. We fight it at first, procrastinate with frequent trips to the refrigerator or mind-numbing Google searches, but when we sit down and let our minds escape that's when the magic begins. The nature conversation is the same. It takes time, it takes concentration, and it means letting go of everything that is swimming inside your mind. And when you take time to listen, when you begin talking to that tree full of wisdom or that lone flower with a smile on its face, it is your newfound friend that sets you free; free to roam inside your own creative epiphany.

MYSTICAL TREES

We all have them, that one tree that beckons our return no matter the age. That one tree that knows all our secrets, where we laughed,

cried and fell in love. It is our forever confident, the gatekeeper of everything near and dear to us. Some are fortunate to see it grow while others mourn its loss.

Be it forested mountains draped in fog or dark forbidding forests, it is the root of creativity, fodder for fairy-tales and even blockbuster movies. There's more than science, health and beauty of trees, as the title of this book implies it is the magical world from whence they live.

Photo by Debojyoti Dey, Sandakphu, the highest point of the Singalila Ridge on the West Bengal-Nepal India border

Some of our most creative books have captured that magic in very intriguing ways. *The Wood Between the Worlds*, the sixth book in the *Chronicles of Narnia* by C. S. Lewis, gives life to a shrouded forest with glistening pools said to be magical portals to other worlds. The woods themselves invite a mystical feel as the tree ceiling is thick with overlapping leafy crowns, but yet there is a warm gold light offering peace and harmony.

The book, *A Game of Thrones* written by George R. R. Martin, was the first novel in the author's *A Song of Ice and Fire* series of five fantasy novels. Inspired by the award-winning books there came a hugely popular television adaption titled, *Game of Thrones*. There are several kingdoms in the series, and some of them are privileged to have a Weirwood tree affectionately called the heart tree. Similar to the North American white pine, it has a stout trunk dressed in a white bark, but the Weirwood tree has blood-red leaves. They have hearts and faces carved in the bark with streams of red falling from the eyes. It is said the Children of the Forest, a non-human race that once lived vicariously in the thick Weirwood forests, carved the faces.

Human invaders called the First Men descended into this wooded Shangri La and began killing the trees, cutting them down with a vengeance. After 2,000 years of fighting, the Children of the Forest created the Night King, a wicked leader of the White Walkers, a zombie-like army, to help eradicate the First Men. But thousands of years later, the Night King and his White Walkers decided to take over the world themselves. However, one of the Weirwood trees has a special power, a force the Night King cannot conquer, and the tree has a prince, Bran Stark, that shares its vision. Another battle is brewing, and how spectacular it would be if this mystical Weirwood would be the ultimate weapon in defeating its foe.

Amazing how a fictional world filled with multiple kingdoms mimic our environmental fights today. Rather than the Night King and White Walkers, the villains of today's world are the greedy developers and capitalists.

The *Lord of the Rings* volumes of books was written by J. R. R. Tolkien, it is an epic fantasy of life in the Middle-earth. Although the books hold their just rewards, the blockbuster movies have an international following that delves deep inside the center of the earth. It is a land filled with men, elves, hobbits and dwarves set in a scene reminiscent of an English countryside hundreds of years ago before the ravage of industrialization.

The movies are filmed in the New Zealand North Island and South Island locations set in everything from a lush dairy farm to mountain ranges covered with enchanting forests. Many scenes of the movies are filmed along snowcapped mountains and the breathtaking Waiau

River flanked by the emerald colored mountains covered by Fanghorn Forest known in the movie as Fangorn Forest.

Lord of the Rings film location Twelve Mile Delta, New Zealand. Photo by Oren Rozen courtesy of Wikimedia Commons

And so the mystery comes to life, no fake fantasy shots, instead it's an eye-opening visit to another world; one that many of us never knew existed. It is *Lord of the Rings: The Two Towers* that bring us inside the Fangorn Forest, let's take a peek and watch the magic.

The scene begins in an ancient forest, a dark, dank forest, almost lifeless with no sound. Two hobbits, Merry and Pippin escape into Fangorn Forest but are in grave danger chased by a soldier of the wicked army of Isengard. The hobbits climb a giant tree believing they are safe until the evil soldier pulls Merry down to the ground. Just as the gruesome soldier draws his sword to strike, the ancient tree comes to life.

His name is Treebeard, the oldest of the tree creatures called Ents. Treebeard pulls his roots from the dirt and smashes the evil soldier. Soon the hobbits are in the tree's branch-like hands and mesmerized that the tree can talk.

Treebeard introduces himself and his tribe, and Merry replies quite smitten, "A tree herder, a shepherd of the forest?" The hobbits then ask what side is he on, and the brilliant dialog begins. "I am on nobody's side because nobody's on my side, nobody cares for the woods anymore."

As the tree carries the two dwarf-size men, they walk out of the forest to a wasteland of stumps and broken limbs, nothing but a field of death and despair.

Treebeard is terribly distraught and says with a shaky voice, "Many of these trees were my friends, creatures I had known from nuts and acorns. They had voices of their own."

Against a garish backdrop, Treebeard lets out an earthy battle cry and wakes the army of the Ents. Leafless and grey they march in war seeking revenge for the fallen trees. In another scene, it is said the trees have great power, full of memory and anger. They have awakened and ready to fight.

It is movies like this that speak the truth, that give us hope and introduce us to a real-life fantasy world. Perhaps movies like this offer more than entertainment; they bring education and preservation.

ECLIPSE ARTISTRY

Imagine the outdoors as a new brand of theater, an endless performance of our living forests. Each creature plays their part, from the ring-tailed raccoons nibbling on their crawfish to the chubby-cheeked chipmunks scouring the forest floor. There's sound too, the operatic cries of sparrows and blue jays pierce the sky while the wind ebbs and flows in a chorus of violins. It is the wind that moves the forest; the branches bend and sway with the finesse of a ballerina while the leaves leap for joy in tune with a giddy tap dancer.

Nature is the greatest stage on earth, and on August 21, 2017, millions of people took to the open fields, forested parkways, and their own backyard to witness another one of nature's most rare and spectacular performances, a total solar eclipse.

To be clear, a solar eclipse occurs during a new moon and requires a direct lineup of the sun, moon and earth. The moon is between the sun and the earth and casts a shadow on the planet. According to the Astronomy Magazine, if you are in the dark part of that shadow you will see a total eclipse, if you are in the light part, you will see a partial eclipse. And of course the sky is just the backdrop. With little or no knowledge of astronomy, most don't really care about the schematics; it's all about being there.

NASA scientists note that the last time the United States was privileged to see the path of a total solar eclipse stretch across the country was one hundred years ago, and the last time it was visible exclusively only to the continental United States was 1776. That's 241 years ago and I certainly doubt there were millions of people wearing their protective eyeglasses.

People along a seventy-mile-wide path from Oregon to South Carolina enjoyed a complete blackout, turning day into night. Although not everyone saw a blackout, the entire country did witness some form of the moon passing over the sun. For example, in my home base of south Louisiana, we saw a crescent-shaped eclipse.

In her award-winning essay, Annie Dillard's classic, "Total Eclipse" paints a surreal picture of the February 1979 total solar eclipse. A champion of the creative spirit, and at times overly blunt, she professed in her essay, "Seeing a partial eclipse bears the same relation to seeing a total eclipse as kissing a man does to marrying him."

Yakima Peak & Tips Lake, Washington. Photo by Ron Clausen

With that, I thought it proper to share her story opposed to my viewing of what she declares is a seemingly incomplete eclipse. Based on her assessment, I have to wholeheartedly agree and hope to view the next total eclipse in April 2024.

Dillard and her husband, Gary, ventured to central Washington near the town of Yakima, Washington. Coursing their way through the Cascades Mountain Range, part of the Pacific range, in what was supposed to be a five-hour trip, they were delayed due to an avalanche that blocked the pass. They had to wait for the highway crews to bull-doze a path through the passage and build a makeshift tunnel with two-by-fours and plywood.

They climbed a 500-foot hill overlooking Yakima valley, what Dillard described as a Shangri-la filled with glowing slopes of orchards. Her prose fills the mind with such detail, such elegance you can almost smell the fruited breeze. A thin shining river, she notes, flowing through the valley with a distant blur and the faint whisper of blue. Behind them was more sky and lowlands blued by distance, then the pinnacle of it all, Mount Adams. Shaped, as Dillard commanded, "like a snow-covered volcanic cone rising flat."

As the sun continued to rise so did the number of people on the hills, as if everyone was there to witness the end of time. Even Dillard remarked they all looked like they just crawled out of spaceships with their heavy garb and nylon parkas. Everyone was focused but oddly there was complete silence, no fireworks or starting gun, and then a small piece of the sun disappeared. Looking through welder's goggles, a scary scene in what Dillard explains is watching the sun going through phases, more like shaved rather than gobbled up.

In her signature style of imagery she sets the scene and in her blatant style of confession, she brings forth a philosophical examination of life. It was her vivid descriptions, setting the scene not only in color but its drama as well.

Writers exhaustively search for new ways to describe the sky, and as usual, Dillard takes a different route. More of what it's not, then what it is. You can feel the momentum building, you can see what she is seeing, the sky was a blue with no darkness, an indigo she recalled, but a color she had never seen before.

And who would have imagined painting a vivid mountain scene in metallics? The world, the grasses, they were all wrong, she said, a platinum color, but dull, like something that has never been seen on earth.

She went on to use metaphors, like a faded color used in a movie filmed in the Middle Ages. Of course there is no such thing, but you can still imagine. Because it was so surreal, it was indeed otherworldly.

Looking at her husband, he seemed distorted, and again she harkened back to a time centuries ago, like "the other side of death."

She continued to use death as her base of discovery, a place no one really sees but only imagines. A feeling, but yet she could hear the screams across the hills, and just as the totality took place, there was silence. No sound, no world, she said, "dead people rotating and orbiting...embedded in the planet's crust."

It was as if the hilltops of Yakima was a massive graveyard, not in horror, not in literal terms, but that unearthly dimension as if everyone stole away a piece of eternity.

Humans have always had an infatuation with both partial and total eclipses. According to the NASA Eclipse website, for thousands of years civilizations across the world believed solar eclipses were a sign from the gods of virtual doom. Many held human and animal sacrifices while others prayed or took shelter.

There is no evidence that a solar eclipse has any direct physical effects on humans unless of course, you view the show with the naked eye. It can then damage your retina in what's called solar retinopathy and provided there are no pain receptors in the retina, the damage is often not detected until it's too late to save your vision.

So while the humans are well aware of what is happening, the plants and animals are a bit confused. Dependent on your location, many of the animals thought it was nighttime. The Science News magazine noted that during an eclipse the usual nocturnal animals such as owls and bats emerge from their daytime roosts while the daytime animals seem a bit spooked or confused.

Farmers report cows and horses return to their barns thinking it's time to begin bedding for the night. There's often an eerie silence as birds stop singing and squirrels along with other animals hide in the dark shadows of the forest. Bees return to their hives, spiders take down their webs, and even pets may be a bit more needy or take refuge in their favorite hiding space.

But the trees literally bring on a whole new light. Sunlight bounces off of trees all the time, and we often take notice of the unique shadows. The eclipse artistry takes place when circles of sunlight squeeze between the leaves. On the day of the eclipse, overlapping leaves created natural pinholes. As the light filtered through the leaves it created mini-eclipse replicas scattered across the ground, houses and roads.

It's a whole new dimension of art with varying shapes and sizes of the crescents. Even the size and species of the tree affects the artwork. The palm tree has an almost pie shape canvas of repeated crescents while the shadows of light filtered through a maple tree resemble fish swimming in an ocean.

One of my favorites is a photo of a shaded walking path flanked by a tunnel of trees. A deluge of multi-layered crescents spills across the asphalt creating what appear to be waves of water. Bound together the slivers of light resemble a mountain stream flowing through a bed of rocks.

In an attempt to create my own eclipse abstracts I positioned my camera on a tripod and experimented with various camera settings. The result is quite captivating as the sun, clouds, and particles of the atmosphere combined to create a jeweled portrait. Zooming in closer reveals the intense beauty of nature, in this case, celestial bands of light.

Studying its symmetry the crescent floats in the confines of a blue mass, similar to the same deep blue in the eye of a hurricane. The partial eclipse casts varying rays of light, thick and thin, some white while others filled with the prisms of a rainbow. Gold orbs reach out to the edge of the photograph in what could best be described as an immortal stairway to heaven.

There are arguments by several groups that there is a form of lunar lunacy. Some experience extreme stress or feeling out of sorts, especially those in tuned with the natural world. Although most scientists don't believe there is overwhelming evidence of such behavior, there is one phenomenon; it brings people together. Millions of people were mesmerized and hypnotized by this astronomical wonder.

Perhaps similar to ancient tribes, it was pure instinct to come together and pay homage to the mysteries of this magnificent planet. Let's hope we can continue this journey in growing our earthly alliance.

❀ 9 ❀

VISIONARY BUCKET LIST

Hoh Rain Forest, Olympic National Park, Washington. Photo by Michael Gäbler

"If we surrendered to earth's intelligence we could rise up rooted, like trees." – Rainer Maria Rilke, Poet & Novelist born in Prague, Bohemia, Austria-Hungary. Died at the age of 51, December 4, 1875-December 29, 1926.

Perhaps only writers can fully understand the psychological quag-mire that haunts us all. We are hypersensitive to the world around us, and without this heightened sensitivity and passion, I would not be a writer. A precious gift, one that should never be denied or tethered too tightly, often consumed with an overactive imagination and the overreaching desire to change the world.

Nature writing especially unravels the neatly tied knot in the pit of my stomach, easing the pain but clearly only the medicine, as the cure is a seriously deep immersion into a native wonderland.

One could say my creative life began in my exhaustive curiosity of the world around me. From climbing trees to the never-ending walks in the woods, I was drawn to nature's ever-changing stage.

My first camera was an Argus Seventy-Five given to me at the age of six, most likely the seed of my creative career. In the 70s, it continued with a Ricoh 35mm camera, then several digital cameras over the last seventeen years with my latest, the Canon 7D. My quest to capture natural landscapes has never wavered in what has become a forty-year passion and career.

A student of Ansel Adams photographs, I hope to instill both the spiritual awakening these images bring and to intensify the emotional drama of today's reality. To inspire, to engage and continue the lessons learned from the greats that came before me.

And so begins a spiritual sojourn, a desire to seek and share the beauty of the world, its natural form captured in multiple landscapes. The forests of Europe and America, interviews with those who live there, those who wish to live silent, to listen only to nature's call. A travelogue, a teaching tool much like this book, my dream destina-tions in a visionary bucket list. One that will begin very soon.

Photo by Malene Thyssen, featuring a wooded pasture
shaped by grazing animals in Langa, Denmark on a cold
January day with frosted mist.
http://www.visitdenmark.com/north-zealand/nature/exploring-
north-zealands-beaches-forests-and-lakes

Photo by Malene Thyssen, featuring new leaves emerging on
a beech tree in Grib Forest. Denmark's fourth largest forest,
it's in the northern part of Sealand and part of UNESCO World
Heritage Site.
http://www.visitdenmark.com/denmark/attractions/unesco-
world-heritage-sites-denmark

Roman Boed, photographer, Black Forest stream near Baiersbronn. The Black Forest is a mountainous region in southwest Germany, bordering France. https://www.black-forest-travel.com/baiersbronn/

Photo by Richard Fabi, Windbeeches on the Schauinsland in Germany's Black Forest. Thick with growth it enjoys lower temperatures and higher rainfall compared to the highlands of the forest. http://www.blackforest-tourism.com/Black-Forest

Horseshoe Falls in Mt Field National Park, Tasmania, Australia. Photo by Ben Weatherhead courtesy of Wikimedia Commons. The first national park in Tasmania, Australia, Mount Field is one of the region's most beloved natural attractions. http://waterfallsoftasmania.com.au/index.php#about

Photo by Michael Gäbler. The Hoh Rainforest in Olympic National Park in Oregon is one of the finest remaining examples of a temperate rainforest in the United States. https://www.nps.gov/olym/planyourvisit/visiting-the-hoh.htm

Photo provided by the park. The nation's largest national forest, the Tongass National Forest covers most of Southeast Alaska, www.fs.usda.gov/tongass/

Photo by King of Hearts courtesy of Wikimedia Commons. A photo of the Valley View of Yosemite National Park. http://www.nps.gov/yose/index.htm

Adirondack Park Forest Preserve, New York, photo by IDA Writer. Said to be
the largest publicly protected area in the contiguous United States.
http://visitadirondacks.com/about/adirondack-park

Photo by Jesse Lee Tucker, Walden Pond State Reservation
designated as a National Historic Landmark. The park shares
the same experience that inspired Henry David Thoreau to
pen his book, Walden.
www.nps.gov/nr/travel/massachusetts_conservation/walden_pond.html

Photo by Redwood National park. These wooded temples
come together in a cathedral of trees sweeping the clouds
rising hundreds of feet into the air.
https://www.nps.gov/redw/index.htm

Photo taken by Jim Bahn. General Sherman tree in the Giant
Forest of Sequoia National Park, CA.
https://www.nps.gov/seki/index.htm

10

TRAVEL NOTES

Abandoned school house on country road in Reliance, Tennessee located in Polk County inside East Tennessee. https://www.tnvacation.com/east-tennessee/reliance

M y quest in sharing the beauty of nature begins in discovering multiple landscapes, with that comes the magic of my words and the essence of my photographs. This book is as much a travelogue as a teaching tool, and I welcome all to experience the same beauty.

Listed below are cities and landscapes featured in this book. I have had the privilege of visiting, reporting and photographing each location. Get lost in nature, carry the forest deep inside you and let the magic begin.

Apalachicola, Florida, www.apalachicolabay.org

Atchafalaya Basin, Louisiana, www.louisiana-
destinations.com/atchafalaya-basin-swamp.htm

Hot Springs, www.hotsprings.org

Jean Lafitte National Historical Park and Preserve, 504-689-
3690, www.nps.gov/jela/barataria-preserve.htm

Livingston Parish Tourism, near the state capital of Baton Rouge,
225-567-7899, www.livingstontourism.com

Louisiana Northshore, www.louisiananorthshore.com

St Tammany Parish Lakefront. Louisiana Travel Tourism,
http://www.louisianatravel.com/

New Mexico, Kasha-Katuwe Tent Rocks National Monument, 505-761-8700,
www.blm.gov

Enchanted Rock, Fredericksburg, TX
http://www.visitfredericksburgtx.com/attractions-activities/enchanted-rock-
state-natural-area/

New Orleans Basin Street Station Visitor Information & Cultural Center, 504-293-2600, http://basinststation.com, New Orleans Regional Transit Authority (RTA), www.norta.com

New Orleans Audubon Park, 1-800-774-7394,
www.audubonnatureinstitute.org/audubon-park

New Orleans City Park, 504-483-9376, www.neworleanscitypark.com

New Orleans Brechtel Park, www.nola.gov/parks-and-parkways/parks-squares/brechtel-park/

New York Central Park, 212-310-6600, http://www.centralparknyc.org/

Roanoke Valley Convention & Visitors Bureau, www.visitroanokeva.com. Blue
Ridge Parkway Association, www.blueridgeparkway.org

Rocky Mountain National Park, Colorado, 970-586-1206,
www.nps.gov/romo/index.htm

Steamboat Springs, www.steamboat.com, 970-879-6111

Washington, D.C., 202-789-7000, https://washington.org/

Fall at the Capital of Washington, D.C.

EPILOGUE

Fox Hound Trail lookout on the Blue Ridge Parkway in Virginia

S everal chapters of this book proclaim my love for nature, and some share my frustration with greed in slaughtering forests for material gain. Perhaps in a world that seems more connected to cell phones rather than political causes, people are finally coming together to protest. Coming together to fight for our environment, to save our trees.

Countries with varying political persuasions are doing the same, developing legislation to protect forests, especially the ancient forests. From Europe to the Americas, national parks and nature preserves are enacting stronger restrictions.

We have lost a great deal of the old-growth forests, some countries will never know such a thing and why it is so critical we work tirelessly to save the few that remain. All of us can begin with our own backyards and stop the relentless spraying of chemicals.

Why do you need grass? Only to watch it grow and complain you must mow it with pollution causing lawn mowers. Start by only tearing down enough trees to build your house and leave the rest alone.

Perhaps it's time we treat our trees like we treat animals. In addition to the increasing numbers of families with pets, the passion for wild animals has also gained more traction. Case in point was the death of Cecil the lion by a trophy hunter in July 2015. The story sparked protests in tribes of loving hearts around the world.

Imagine the same outrage if an ancient tree were cut down? It would go viral on social media, photos of the tree in its natural environment and the hungry machines tearing apart its limbs, amputating its crown and decimating its roots and brains. Yes, there would be an outrage for sure.

Scientists have proved that pets help make humans happier, less stressed, a reason to keep living. And we lovingly look out at our gardens, woods and national forest preserves, how many realize our forests do the same?

Education is the key, and hopefully reading this book, along with many others noted will help ignite more preservation. We must come together, fight for our trees because we are their voice in a world of woe.

Photo above is a towering tree in Mount Rainier National Park, photo by Tobias Haase. Some cast snide comments against the crazy tree-huggers but we are one with the trees, one with nature. Yes we need lumber, but we could grow trees on a tree farm and leave the natural forests alone. Like humans, these trees need to pass down their knowledge to future generations in order to survive.

In the last chapter of *The Hidden Life of Trees*, the book points out that the entire country of Switzerland is dedicated to maintaining the "green species." Their constitution reads, "account {is} to be taken of the dignity of creation when handling animals, plants and other organisms."

It's a perfect example of inducing an emotional bond with green space and subsequently a more tolerant behavior of both plants and animals. The key word is emotional, which is a hard word to swallow for lumber industries.

But there is hope, environmental groups and forest users are communicating. It's critical that everyone see forests as the future. Thousands of species living together, interwoven and interdependent, a harmonious ecosystem dedicated to building a growing forest for future generations. We are all interconnected.

Proof positive is a story from Japan that forester/author Peter Wohlleben used to close his book. A marine chemist from a Japanese university discovered that leaves falling into local streams leach acids into the ocean that stimulates the growth of plankton. This in turns provides more food for fish. They began planting more trees in coastal areas which lead to higher production by both fisheries and oyster growers.

More reasons why we should all continue to save our trees; continue to dream away under their branches and continue our love affair with these majestic creatures. Keep walking the woods my friend, keep talking to the trees and asking those hard questions. And one day, one day they will answer.

ABOUT THE AUTHOR

A confessed tree-hugger, Deborah Burst is enamored with the mystical world of nature. Equally passionate about history and preservation, she travels to what seems to be the ends of the earth. It's her addiction, be it spying a hidden graveyard, opening the doors to another sacred temple, or scouring the dark corners of shrouded bayous and forests, Burst gives a voice to all the spirits.

As an award-winning writer and photographer, she has written five books in five years. Her birthplace of New Orleans was the impetus for her first book and the matriarch in the Sacred Places legacy. The city's sanctuaries, cemeteries and oak-filled parks will forever have a home in her work.

That is her mission: to bring passion and purpose to the page, to share both the beauty and the reality.

Deborah Burst is available for speaking events with her colorful collage of photographs combined with an animated presentation.

You can contact her at debswriting@hotmail.com, or via social media on Facebook under her full name, Deborah Burst, or Twitter @debburst.

Print books are available via the author's website along with her blog, published articles and photo galleries

www.deborahburst.com

debswriting@hotmail.com

BIBLIOGRAPHY

Bibliography

100% Pure New Zealand website. *The Lord of the Rings Trilogy Filming Locations.* http://www.newzealand.com/us/feature/the-lord-of-the-rings-trilogy-filming-locations/ (accessed August 24, 2017)

ABC 7 Eyewitness News. *What makes this eclipse so rare? And more facts and figures.* http://abc7chicago.com/weather/facts-that-will-get-you-excited-for-the-eclipse/2272582/ (accessed September 9, 2017)

Astronomy magazine. *25 Facts you should know about the August 21, 2017, total solar eclipse.* http://cs.astronomy.com/asy/b/astronomy/archive/2014/08/05/25-facts-you-should-know-about-the-august-21-2017-total-solar-eclipse.aspx (accessed September 10, 2017)

Beal, C.A. *Be a Tree: the Natural Burial Guide for Turning Yourself into a Forest.* April 10, 2016. Be a Tree, http://www.beatree.com/ (accessed April 10, 2016).

Ben Raines. *The Underwater Forest.* http://www.al.com/news/mobile/index.ssf/2017/06/underwater_forest_discovered_alabama.html (accessed August 19, 2017)

Biography Website. *John Muir.*

https://www.biography.com/people/john-muir-9417625   (accessed
August 9, 2017)

Biography   Website.   *Thomas*   *Edison.*
https://www.biography.com/people/thomas-edison-9284349
(accessed August 19, 2017)

Brooks, Rebecca Beatrice. *The Life of Henry David Thoreau.* History of
Massachusetts Blog. http://historyofmassachusetts.org/henry-david-
thoreau/ (accessed August 21, 2017)

Cedar Tree Healing Arts website. *Nature as a spiritual path: Six sugges-*
tion   for   deepening   your   spiritual   relationship   to   Nature.
http://www.cedartreehealing.org/blog/2014/12/5/nature-as-a-
spiritual-path-six-suggestions-for-deepening-your-spiritual-
relationship-to-nature (Accessed October 5, 2017)

City   Park   Blog.   *Keep   the   Oak   Trees   Safe.*
http://neworleanscitypark.com/blog/keep-the-oak-trees-safe
(accessed September 4, 2017)

City Park. *City Park is one of the oldest urban parks in the country.*
http://neworleanscitypark.com/about (accessed June, 4, 2017)

City   Park.   *New   Orleans   City   Park   History.*
http://neworleanscitypark.com/new-orleans-city-park-history
(accessed June 4, 2017)

Dillard, Annie. *Pilgrim at Tinker Creek.* New York, New York. Harper-
Perennial, Modern Classics. January 1974

Energy and Environmental Affairs website. *Walden Pond State Reser-*
vation.   http://www.mass.gov/eea/agencies/dcr/massparks/region-
north/walden-pond-state-reservation.html (accessed August 20, 2017)

Fandom   website.   *Game   of   Thrones   Wiki,   Weirwood.*
http://gameofthrones.wikia.com/wiki/Weirwood (accessed September
9, 2017)

Fandom   website.   *Wood   Between   the   Worlds.*
http://narnia.wikia.com/wiki/Wood_Between_the_Worlds   (accessed
August 23, 2017)

Higgins, Richard. *THOREAU and the LANGUAGE of TREES.* California. University of California Press. 2017.

Inside Climate News. *California Fires: Record Hot Summer, Wet Winter*

Created Explosive Mix. https://insideclimatenews.org/news/10102017/fires-napa-sonoma-california-climate-change-worst-wildfire-season (Accessed October 16, 2017)

Inside Climate News. *Cost of Climate Change: Early Estimate for Hurricanes, Fires reaches $300 Billion.* https://insideclimatenews.org/news/28092017/hurricane-maria-irma-harvey-wildfires-damage-cost-estimate-record-climate-change (Accessed October 16, 2017)

Mark, Jason. *Get Out of Here: Scientists Examine the Benefits of Forests, Birdsong and Running Water.* March 2, 2017.

Met Website. *Jackson Pollock.* http://www.metmuseum.org/art/collection/search/488978 (accessed August 10, 2017)

NASA Total Eclipse. *Eclipse 101.* https://eclipse2017.nasa.gov/faq (accessed September 10, 2017)

National Park Service website. *Muir Woods.* https://www.nps.gov/muwo/index.htm (accessed August 22, 2017)

National Recreation and Park Association. *Creating a Vibrant Public Space on the Lafitte Greenway.* http://www.nrpa.org/parks-recreation-magazine/2017/august/creating-a-vibrant-public-space-on-the-lafitte-greenway/ (Accessed October 8, 2017)

Reiher, Andrea. *Game of Thrones: Why Weirwood Trees May Be the Key to Defeating the Undead.* https://www.popsugar.com/entertainment/What-Weirwood-Trees-Game-Thrones-43878168 (accessed August 23, 2017)

Roosevelt, Theodore. Sierra Club website. *John Muir: An Appreciation.* http://vault.sierraclub.org/john_muir_exhibit/life/appreciation_by_roosevelt.aspx (accessed August 22, 2017)

Schneider, Richard, J. *Life and Legacy Thoreau's Life.* http://www.thoreausociety.org/life-legacy (accessed August 20, 2017).

Sierra Club website. *Theodore Roosevelt.* http://vault.sierraclub.org/john_muir_exhibit/people/roosevelt.aspx (accessed August 22, 2017)

Sierra Club website. *Chapter IX, The Sequoia and General Grant National* *Parks.* http://vault.sierraclub.org/john_muir_exhibit/writings/our_national_parks/chapter_9.aspx (Accessed October 28, 2017)

Simard, Suzanne. *Do Trees Communicate.* July 29, 2012. Do Trees Communicate, https://www.youtube.com/watch?v=iSGPNm3bFmQ (accessed March 21, 2016).

The Atlantic magazine website. Annie Dillard's Classic Essay: 'Total Eclipse.' August 8, 2017. https://www.theatlantic.com/science/archive/2017/08/annie-dillards-total-eclipse/536148/ (Accessed October 10, 2017)

The Atlantic magazine website. *The Health Benefits of Trees.* July 29, 2014. https://www.theatlantic.com/health/archive/2014/07/trees-good/375129/ (Accessed October 5, 2017).

The Nature Conservancy. *Natural Climate Solutions.* https://global.nature.org/initiatives/natural-climate-solutions/natures-make-or-break-potential-for-climate-change (Accessed October 17, 2017)

The Trust for Public Land. *New Orleans Will Add First New Park to City in 20 Years.* https://www.tpl.org/media-room/new-orleans-will-add-first-new-park-city-20-years#sm.0001lsfl48plocs5pzn2m7hjhfnom (Accessed October 8, 2017)

The Trust for Public Land. *Ten Years after Katrina, a new chapter for New Orleans parks.* https://www.tpl.org/blog/ten-years-after-katrina-a-new-chapter-for-new-orleans-parks#sm.0001lsfl48plocs5pzn2m7hjhfnom (Accessed October 8, 2017)

The Weather Channel. *Atlantic Hurricane Season 2017, Now Seventh Most Active in History.* https://weather.com/en-CA/canada/news/news/2017-10-09-atlantic-hurricane-season-one-of-busiest-october (Accessed October 16, 2017)

Turnage, William. *Ansel Adams, Photographer.* http://anseladams.com/ansel-adams-bio/ (accessed August 20, 2017)

Yee, Lawrence. *Games of Thrones: How the Children of the Forest and the First Men Made Peace.* http://fandom.wikia.com/articles/game-of-

thrones-children-of-the-forest-first-men?
li_source=LI&li_medium=wikia-impactfooter (accessed August
23, 2017)

YouTube. *Lord of the Rings: The Two Towers Treebeard.*
https://www.youtube.com/watch?v=BbV2Hr0qRdo (accessed August
23, 2017)

YouTube. *The White Wizard LOTR.*
https://www.youtube.com/watch?v=Dl2R4v9YvEA#t=3.972284
(accessed August 23, 2017)

Wikipedia website. *The Lord of the Rings.*
https://en.wikipedia.org/wiki/The_Lord_of_the_Rings (accessed
August 24, 2017)

Wikipedia website. *Wood between the Worlds*
https://en.wikipedia.org/wiki/Wood_between_the_Worlds (accessed
August 23, 2017)

Wilkey, Greg, interview by Deborah Burst. Professional educator,
school administrator and published author of YA fiction. (June
7, 2017)

Williams, Florence. *The Nature Fix; Why Nature Makes Us Happier,
Healthier, and More Creative.* New York, New York. W.W. Norton &
Company, Inc. 2017.

Wohlleben, Peter. *The Hidden Life of TREES.* Munich, Germany. Grey-
stone Books. 2016.

WORLD BOOK Website. *6 Weird Effects of a Total Solar Eclipse.*
https://www.worldbooklearning.com/6-weird-effects-of-a-total-solar-
eclipse/ (accessed September 9, 2017)

CPSIA information can be obtained
at www.ICGtesting.com
Printed in the USA
BVOW05s0359131117
500214BV00025B/472/P